Running in Circles

CHASING DREAMS AND DODGING HOT FLASHES

Gillian Stapleton

First published in 2023 by **Putting Words.**
© Gillian Stapleton, 2023
The moral rights of the author have been asserted.

All rights reserved except as permitted under the Australian Copyright Act 1968 (for example, fair dealing for the purposes of study, research, criticism or review). No part of this publication may be reproduced, distributed, or transmitted in any form or by any means, including photocopying, recording, or other electronic or mechanical methods, without the author's prior written permission. All requests should be made through the publisher at the address below.

Putting Words
PO Box 5062
Wonga Park,
Victoria, Australia. 3115

www.puttingwords.com
books@puttingwords.com

A catalogue record for this book is available from the National Library of Australia.

ISBN: 978-0-6456666-0-1 (Paperback)

Produced by **Putting Words**
Cover Design by Ashish Joshi

Gillian Stapleton makes you feel anything is possible. Her stories of competing and of the friendships that she's made through her running will have you pulling on your fitness gear and heading for the door. What comes through though in Running in Circles is the encouragement to accept that everyone starts from somewhere and while the hurdles ahead might sometimes seem insurmountable, in the end, just starting the journey can sometimes be all it takes.

Lisa Millar
ABC Journalist.

Runners are good people.

In all my years of running, I have come to the realisation that "ratbags" don't run.

Running is hard, but it can also be the most rewarding and fulfilling thing you can do. Nothing else is as simple but also as challenging as running.

This beautiful life story and journey by Gillian Stapleton highlights one runner's struggles and triumphs, both in running and in life and connects us with her running family.

As runners, we are all connected. We understand the disappointment of injury and illness, the challenges of the marathon (or your first 5k), the thrills and joys of a Personal Best and the friendships forged through shared sweat and toil.

Running is one of the most powerful things anyone can do. It requires virtually no equipment; you can do it alone or with your best friends and you can do it anywhere across the globe.

It is not only beneficial for our physical health but a powerful medicine for our mental health, well-being and self-esteem. I see this every day through the work I do with my not-for-profit charity, The Indigenous Marathon Foundation and the powerful and positive transformation that our First Nations runners go through, especially when they run their first marathon is extraordinary.

Congratulations, Gillian, on the insight, you have provided and shared with your readers and I know this book will inspire others also to pull on the Asics, get off the couch and grow as individuals, friends and family.

We may run in circles ending up back where we started, but when we get back, we are not the same person we were.

If you want to be inspired, hang out with runners.

Rob de Castella AO MBE

Uplifting, engaging, motivating.

Running in Circles: Chasing Dreams and Dodging Hot Flashes is a refreshingly open and wonderfully written book and Gillian's warmth and relatability had me "lacing up my runners" and "running with her" from the very first chapter.

And what plays out among the pages, from the early days of Gillian's running to her training, through all the incredible marathons and life in between is a deeply personal journey of resilience, friendship, family love and support, resourcefulness and a rediscovery of purpose in life.

There are so many messages to take away from this book. But what I particularly love is that it confirms this quiet truth – that the positive impact of running goes far beyond simply running itself.

It is life-changing. Life-affirming. Empowering.

I know this beautiful book will inspire you too.

Heather Hawkins
Adventurer

Running is like life. There are highs and lows in the journey of life, just as there are highs and lows in running a marathon. There are so many parallels with life's lessons that are to be found in Gillian's inspiring, motivating and empowering book. With every chapter of her book, Gillian shares pearls of wisdom; she shares the joys and the pain as she runs around the world.

Behind each race, there is grit, determination, beauty, strength and challenges that are so understood by anyone who has dared train for a marathon. Running in Circles is for all the marathoners out there and for all those who have ever dreamt of running 5, 10, 21, 42 km or more.

This book is an eloquent reminder that running gives us resilience, community, family and an ability to believe in ourselves and others. It is a reminder that running is so much more profound than putting one foot in front of the other – it can be a panacea for many of the mental and physical ailments that are part of being human.

Congratulations to Gillian for becoming the author of a beautiful book – that shows us life really does begin after 40 or even 47.

Annie Crawford AO
Founder Can Too

From her first race in Paris in 2009, raising money for Can Too, completing the World Marathon Majors, to her most recent triumphs running trail races and ultra-races, Gillian's determination and strength positively shine through on every page.

Her commitment to her family, her friends and her running community is a reward for everyone who has been a part of Gillian's story.

Travelling Fit has been a small part of her journey and being able to help in achieving her goal of running in Tokyo was an opportunity we simply could not pass up.

We look forward to sharing many more adventures together and being as inspired by the next 15 years of running as we have been by reading about the last 15.

Mari-Mar Walton
Travelling Fit Founder and Director

> Turns out it was not the distance of the marathon or the time it took.
>
> The two were simply tools to find that 'something' inside yourself.
>
> You do not run a marathon to stop feeling or run away from a feeling
>
> You run a marathon to feel something and find something inside yourself.
>
> Helen Carmody
> (Gillian's marathon partner)

Running in Circles

Chasing Dreams and Dodging Hot Flashes

"Quaintrelle"

A woman

who prioritises a life full of

Passion

Inspiration

and

Pleasure

To my soul mate, Chad

You have always been my rock. Steady and supportive in all that I do. Your unwavering love and encouragement mean the world to me.

This book is dedicated to you with all my love and gratitude.

Contents

Introduction 1

2009 Paris Marathon 5

2010 New York Marathon # 1 19

2011 Berlin Marathon 31

2012 London Marathon 44

2013 Boston Marathon #1 53

2013 Chicago Marathon 65

2014 Boston Marathon #2 74

2015 Melbourne Marathon 86

2017 San Francisco Marathon 98

2017 New York Marathon #2 108

2019 Tokyo Marathon 124

2022 Canberra Marathon 134

Conclusion - The Ripple Effects of Running 144

Acknowledgements 153

About the Author 154

Introduction

Discover the life-changing power of running 12 Marathons.

I wrote *Running in Circles* for women in their 40s (50s and 60s) who want to claim back a little time for themselves and significantly improve their mental and physical well-being, for women who want to thrive through menopause and want to keep moving forward.

Why running? I was lucky when I found my passion for running at age 47. For you, it might not be running, but this book will inspire you to find an activity that will make you want to move more.

Moving more will help you thrive through menopause. It will positively impact your Mental and Physical well-being.

It will make you smile, shed a tear and stir you into being more active, making new friends and managing work and life better.

This book will inspire you because it is authentic. It is real, raw and relatable. It is my personal story.

Post-COVID many women 40+ have been very focused on juggling all things family, home-schooling and career, neglecting their physical and mental health.

This book will motivate you to take back control of your own body and have a positive long-term effect on your health and well-being.

Much has been written about the three M's – Menopause, Mental Health and Marathons but little has been written that combines all three. *Running in Circles* will motivate and inspire you to take control and claim back your life at home and in the workplace. I am a Mum, a Wife, a CEO, post-menopausal and a Marathon Runner.

My mission is to help disrupt your "okay-ness" with the ordinary and restore your zest for life by inspiring you to find your passion and purpose to move.

This book is simple to read. It follows a real story of a real woman (me) who needed more in her life than just work and family. Running 12 Marathons, including the Boston Marathon when the bomb exploded, taught me how to bounce back from adversity, overcome barriers and live life to the full.

I am 60 + now, but that is simply a number to me. Neither age nor menopause defines me.

I have completed twelve marathons in the past 13 years (COVID stopped 13 in 13).

I started running at the young age of 47. I had spent seven years as a wife, mother and CEO following our move to Australia, settling children into school and life, building a new career and making new friends.

All were much harder than I had anticipated.

I enjoyed my 40s. Life changed direction when my family emigrated from the UK. The children were doing well, my husband was enjoying his new job and we loved our new life in Sydney.

But something was missing for me.

I had lost my village community. My sense of self was missing, as I spent all of my energy ensuring the family was happy and my career was thriving.

We chose to leave friends and family behind for a dream role in Australia and seven years on, I still felt it was my responsibility to ensure it all worked.

I joined a charity running group, Can Too, and learnt to run while raising money to help them fund researchers, trying to find a cure for cancer.

When I turned up on the coldest night of the year in Sydney to run around an oval, I had no idea that it was to be one of those moments in time, that changed my path in life. It was the start of my running story and why I have written this book.

I turned to running to carve out some time for myself, to find myself and escape one night a week, just for 12 weeks.

Fifteen years on, running has helped me through some of the most challenging times of my life – my husband's redundancy and stroke, empty nesting, house moves and career changes, the dreaded Menopause, COVID and a sea change.

The ripple effect of my passion for running through my 50s and now 60s, constantly moving my body, has changed me and It may do the same for you.

This is not a technical book; my goal is just to inspire you to move more. Many running books are written about how to run and they know way more than I do, so I will leave that to the experts.

This book is about running later in life, its impact on my mental and physical well-being, my career and the positive effect it had on those around me.

If I can run 12 marathons in 12 years, too many half-marathons to count, build a successful career, raise two amazing adults, move house six times, thrive in Menopause and still be married to the love of my life 40 years on, I consider that I am doing ok.

CHAPTER 1

2009 Paris Marathon

> The medal!
> Who knew a piece of metal hanging on a ribbon could mean so much to me and change me in an instant!

Very few people wake up and decide to run a marathon. I did not and I do not know many who have. I do not know anyone.

There were many pointers along the way (or signs, as I like to call them), but as I look back, so much of what I had achieved in my 30s set me up for marathon running, which I started in my late 40s.

In my 30s, I started a home-based business so that I could work from home with my two small children. Raising children and running a business from home was not easy, but the lessons I learned in that business were life-long and set me up for success in many areas of my life, including marathon running, as you will discover.

Ann, my sales manager, taught me one of these lessons very early on when I was trying to grow the business. I was struggling with imposter syndrome. I looked around and all I could see were successful women, thriving in their businesses. I was overwhelmed by what I knew it must take and questioned myself about my ability to do what they did. A brief conversation about an elephant with Ann changed my approach and has held me in good stead for the past 30 years. The concept may sound simple, but it can be challenging to do.

Ann asked me, "How do you eat an elephant?" I had no idea. She replied, "One bite at a time."

"How do you run a marathon? One step at a time." Breaking down a problem into bite-size pieces has been my mantra for years, at work and in running.

The challenges of running a small business, leading a large multi-national business, completing a marathon training and crossing the finish line of a marathon after 42.195 km, can all be broken down into small bite-size pieces that can be done every day, every hour or minute by minute. This saying has been in my head every day since I first heard it.

I have a gold chain of elephants that I wear around my neck and it acts as my constant reminder. I have run every marathon wearing it, reminding myself that I will make it to the finish line and I will get to wear the marathon medal around my neck if I break the run into bite-size pieces, one step at a time; one foot in front of the other. I look at challenges at work, at home and in my running and then break them down into more manageable tasks, that allows me to take action and not get stuck in procrastination mode.

In my 40s, I was offered a job in Sydney. Emigrating to a new country at 40 and uprooting your husband and two kids is daunting. Life was very different for a while. I spent years adapting to the Australian way of life. The school system was different and who knew Saturdays were spent driving kids to sport all day? I was building a new career, making new friends and learning to do things the "Aussie way." It left little time for me.

Then one day, I was stirred into action by an advertisement on television for the Can Too Foundation. Can Too is an independent health promotion charity committed to funding cancer research. They offer professionally coached sports training programs across NSW and Queensland using qualified and experienced coaches.

Can Too trains all levels, from beginners to more experienced athletes, in structured training programs tailored to specific physical challenges such as running races, ocean swims, trail walking and adventure challenges. The advertisement said they would teach me how to run if I raised money for cancer research. This advertisement changed my life.

Ticking the box of time out for me and appealing to my social conscience, I signed up for a 9 km event with Can Too and drove to the training ground on Sydney's coldest night of the year. I had no idea where I was going, I had no idea what to wear and I knew no one. Rugged up and fearful about running around an oval on a dark night, I decided it was just one step. What was the worst thing that could happen?

I ran a few laps and thought I was going to die. I was very nervous; I was not a runner and the idea of running a 9 km race in just 12 weeks scared me to death. The idea that everyone was also new and scared never crossed my mind. In my mind, it was only me!

Minutes later, having completed four laps of the 400m oval, I was exhausted, breathless and believing that I had made the wrong decision, I was about to bail. The coach that night then explained the warmup was complete and that we were ready for the training. Ready? I was finished. The outcry from the small group of women heartened me. I was not alone. Others were finding it tough. I stayed. An hour later driving home in the car, I knew I would show up for the training the following Saturday, but I had no idea why.

Nervously, I returned the following week with even more layers of clothing on this time, only to find other runners, who had also found it challenging but they had also decided that it was worth the discomfort. Week by week, we were trained to overcome the fear and breathlessness of running by one of the amazing coaches. Her name was Fi. Week by week I slowly improved and the training became a little easier. I met a few like-minded women who were also out of their comfort zone and I began to look forward to the training, on those cold winter nights.

In the following chapters, I will discuss other ways that you can get started with running but for now, trust me when I say it was well worth the first few weeks of pain and anxiety.

Step by step and run by run, I realised that the women in the group shared the same anxieties and fears about finishing the race. I could never have imagined that I could run that far with just 12 weeks of training, running three times a week. If I can do that at the age of 47, I know you can.

We completed three months of training, following a carefully planned schedule that Coach Fi had written. The goal felt enormous, but I was doing it with a group of like-minded people and we had a plan to follow.

Running around the sports oval never seemed to get any easier, but every Wednesday, we ran laps, fast and slow. We learned the language of running and we showed up every Saturday morning for what we now knew, was called "the long run."

We ran in the Blackmores Running Festival just twelve weeks later and we all completed the entire 9 km run.

That day in September 2007, when I crossed the finish line at the steps of Sydney Opera House, a volunteer placed a finishing medal around my neck and I felt like a world champion.

The medal! Who would have thought a piece of metal hanging on a ribbon could mean so much to me and change me in an instant? I had never been great at sports in school and I do not ever remember winning a sporting event, so I was my own champion at that moment. I was ecstatic. I was glowing inside.

My new running buddy, Helen and I crossed the line together. We had met at the cold track that first winter training session and had no idea that this finishing line would be the first of many finishing lines we would cross together and the first of many medals we would achieve running. It was the start of a friendship that would lead to world travel, many marathon finish lines and so much more.

This was just the first of many ripple effects of running.

Feeling like world champions, we had achieved our goal. But completing the 9 km 2007 Blackmores Running Festival in Sydney was the start of something much bigger and that was running the 2009 Paris Marathon.

Looking back at that training now, I realise that the "Saturday long run" was shorter than the runs I do most days of the week now, but at the time, I would arrive on Saturday morning ready to run at 7 am and feel the fear in the pit of my stomach, wondering if I would be able to make the distance. As the weeks passed, a few of us hung around after each training run to grab a coffee and discuss running and the goal ahead.

My running life had begun. Within weeks we returned to the Can Too programme, this time to train for 21.195 km, our first half marathon, the first of many more to come. By now, the coffee catch-ups were a regular feature after each run and we finally decided to meet for dinner one night.

I was making new friends who shared a common goal; I was getting fitter and learning to run. Dinner was quite funny because by now, we thought we had begun to know each other quite well, but that first time in the restaurant was weird. We had never seen each other dressed in anything other than running gear, we had never seen each other in make-up, and never discussed anything other than running.

Since moving to Australia, these friendships formed on running and a shared goal have become some of the most inspirational relationships in my life. They began without the label of wife, mother, colleague, or boss attached to them and more importantly, any judgement of what you wore, how you did your hair or how much money you earned. This meant we were a diverse group, initially of women, who met up to run and then we became a support group for each other as life threw us all sorts of twists and turns. Still, years later, we are there for each other.

As we trained for that half marathon and other running distances, our partners started to join in; some showed up for coffee, and others joined the running events and that was how I came to be in my first running group. Yet another ripple effect of running and possibly the most significant. There are still so many more to share with you, on this journey.

Crossing the finishing line of the Sydney Half Marathon with post-race celebrations in Hyde Park that included champagne, the idea of running a full marathon was sparked. With 21.195 km behind me and another shiny medal around my neck, I began to wonder if a 48+-year-old woman could run a marathon.

As one of six children growing up in the 1960s in the UK, sport was not a significant feature of our lives; in fact, it did not feature at all outside of compulsory Physical Education (PE) at school. That is why that first medal around my neck was so significant. I had never achieved in sport. There were no medals or trophies on a shelf at home.

I remember a time as a teenager when my brother Nigel and I tried to run laps around the recreation ground in front of our house, but it did not last long. That is why I was so surprised to find out, a few years later (before I started running), that my brother was training for the 2002 London Marathon. I was so proud of him; it took him months of training and fundraising for a mate, but he crossed that finish line.

Living in Australia by then, I could not support him, but as I wondered if I could complete a 42.195 km marathon run, I looked to him for inspiration. If he could do it, then maybe so could I.

The idea of running a full marathon was germinating and I realised that the ripple effect of running had started many years before and it was not me who had started it. I blame Nigel.

Helen and I started talking. We were both busy professional women, raising families and juggling careers and life. The Paris Marathon was her idea. Helen decided that if we were going to run just one marathon, it would be stunning!

Helen loved scenic runs and Paris has to be one of the most picturesque cities in the world. We had little idea at this stage what was involved, but we had enlisted the help of the fantastic Coach Fi, who had coached us that first cold night at the oval in 2007.

Training for a marathon would take a lot of time and discipline. We both worried we might give up part way through the training due to time pressures with family and long working hours. The only way we knew to make this happen was to create an unbreakable commitment.

Paris is a long way from Sydney, where we lived and it is expensive to get there. We booked four flights. Our husbands were keen to join us, support our goal and get a free holiday out of our madness. We paid the money; we got an entry and there was no turning back. If running a marathon was not enough, we had committed financially just to be sure we did not let life get in the way. Leaving work on time to get to training, became easier when you looked at the dollar value behind it.

With our training plan written by Coach Fi, she became the first of many members of our marathon support crew over the years. It was very daunting. Looking at the weekly mileage we had to complete and the time commitment, it would have been easy to be overwhelmed. I just had to look at it day by day and week by week. I had to break it down into bite-size pieces.

I found a simple technique that has served me for all the marathons since. Despite commitments at home with two teenagers, school activities and busy home life, I had to fit every session in. Work for both my husband and I involved travel and long hours. Throwing a marathon into the mix was going to take some planning. I diarised every session into my phone. Every session for the full 16 weeks was in my calendar and I made a commitment to myself.

'I could move a training session, but I could never delete it.'

This meant that on some days when work commitments came up, I doubled up with one training in the morning and another in the evening, but the commitment to myself was made and I was going to give it my best shot.

This marathon also needed the support of my family. If I was going to achieve this, they would have to help. As I had learned so many years back when growing my business, big goals have to be a family affair so that we are all invested in the outcome.

Explaining why this was important to me and what I needed in the way of support from all of them made the first steps easier as they took on more around the house. It may sound selfish in some ways, but the ripple effect of my running marathons on my teenagers, would grow over the years but more about when we get to the 2017 New York Marathon chapter.

The training was tough of course, but slowly my body adapted as it realised, I was going to do this and had to step up. Social events dwindled as I struggled to stay awake past 7 pm, but my husband and friends seemed to understand that it was only going to be one marathon and it was only 16 weeks, or so we all thought.

Having gone into this somewhat blindly, we had never considered that the Paris Marathon being held in April would mean summer training in Sydney. Long training runs were getting longer and Helen and I both struggled with the heat. We started earlier and earlier every Saturday morning, trying to avoid the sun, leaving home in the dark, beginning the run before sunrise and questioning what we were thinking and why we were doing this. I will never forget one morning standing on the clifftop looking out over Sydney Harbour, watching the sunrise and wondering if it was all worth it. It was!

The weariness was creeping in. Busy weeks at work and a full training schedule left little room for anything else. Both husbands were amazing and joined our ever-growing support crew by running some of the streets with us or cycling to a spot along the route with cold water and bananas to keep up our energy levels. This was another ripple effect and the support from my husband, Chad, would form part of my training for the years to come.

Meeting up with our new running friends as we finished the long runs was fun and built a strong bond between Helen and me. Some of the running group, by now, had completed a marathon themselves and were able to offer words of encouragement and keep us on track. Others watched from the sidelines to see if running a marathon might be for them one day.

There were many stumbling blocks as we completed the training, not least a few injuries that were part of most marathons, but I will save the stories about these for another chapter!

As we headed to Paris in April 2009, just a 24-hour flight away from Sydney, we were more than nervous. We had no idea what we were in for or if we could even do it, but we had completed the training and were on our way to our first start line.

Race day of a marathon starts with the collection of the race bib which has your competitor's number on it and is pinned to your running shirt. This bib identifies you as a race participant and has a timing chip built into it; this is how they track your finishing time. Generally, you collect the race bib at the expo the day before and that is when it starts to sink in that you are about to attempt to run a distance that most never try and many do not complete. The expo is the marathon running exhibition and it is exciting and nerve-wracking all in one breath.

The running exhibition (expo) has endless running gear and merchandise for sale with branded marathon gear for that particular race. At the expo, you are surrounded by fellow runners and tempted to buy every possible gadget and piece of gear you can get your hands on just in case it might help you cross that finish line. The unwritten golden rule of not trying to run in anything new on race day tends to go out the window. Our first expo was no different to the many that would follow, we would buy loads of new gear that we did not need and we would always buy a race day shirt (or two), but this first running expo stands out for another reason.

Leaving the expo area with our race bib and pins to fix the bib onto our shirt, we also had been given a plastic garbage bag. Whilst this would feature significantly when we ran the Boston Marathon in 2013, we had no idea what it was for. Rubbish maybe? It got left in the hotel room anyway.

Finally, race day arrived. The pre-race rituals and nerves began. Breakfast routines are specific to each runner and should have been practised for weeks. Mine is quite simple and involves bananas, bagels and hot coffee. I got up early to drink coffee and eat in plenty of time to let things settle. Once the endless nervous toilet visits had been completed, Helen and I headed to the start line in the Champs Elysees. It was drizzling a little and we now realised what the garbage bags were for. You were supposed to make a hole in the top and wear it to the start line to stop you from getting wet. What a rookie error!

Mine was still in the hotel room. The second lesson of that day and there were to be many ahead, was that we had to start running on cobblestones. Thinking we were well prepared; this discovery was messing with my head from the start. We had not trained for this, but as I was to learn in all the marathons to follow, you can only prepare for the running part of the marathon. There is so much more to running a marathon than just running. Every marathon would throw in some unplanned event that had to be overcome on the day to reach the finish line.

The Paris Marathon route started near the intersection of Avenue de Champs-Elysées and Rue Marbeuf and Rue du Colisée. We headed downhill along the broad cobblestone expanse toward the Mile 1 marker at the Place de la Concorde and were on our way. Passing by the Louvre and the Tuileries Garden, we headed into the picturesque park of Bois de Vincennes.

We ran the city of Paris. It was absolutely glorious.

Helen and I had an incredible support team that day. Chad and Helen's husband, David, were there with many of my family from the UK. My brother Nigel, who had run the London Marathon many years prior, had hired a minibus and driven some of my family through the Channel Tunnel to watch me run.

They were there on the streets of Paris, cheering us on with flags and banners. Helen and I had decided early on that as we were only going to run one marathon, we would do it in aid of breast cancer. My family waved pink ladies and pink balloons to remind us that we were running for a bigger reason. Steph, my niece, had also made a pink banner that she held u as we ran by. This banner was to feature in many races to come.

This support and their loud cheers kept our spirits up when they got low. Our lowest point was around the 35 km distance. We had run well and enjoyed the day, but our energy was low by this time. The mind games began.

We struggled to wind through the former hunting ground of French kings, Bois de Boulogne which went on for almost 9 km. I got my phone out and started taking crazy pictures to distract my brain from the pain and make Helen laugh. None of them was any good and I have loads of weird side-view photos that do not show anything, but they served a purpose and we kept moving forward, one step at a time. We kept running.

We emerged from the park onto Avenue Foch, just a few hundred metres from the Paris Marathon finish line and we could see the Arc de Triomphe up ahead. The finish line was in sight and it was at this moment that my daughter Shelby, who had flown in from overseas to support me, appeared from nowhere and gave us each a Pink Lady Breast Cancer Banner to carry across the line.

It gave us the final boost of energy and determination that we needed to run those last steps across the cobblestones and cross the finish line of the 2009 Paris Marathon.

Helen and I had made it. We completed the Paris Marathon at the age of 49.

Helen had previously said to me once, "You do not run a marathon to stop feeling or run away from a feeling. You run a marathon to feel something and find something inside yourself."

I felt something change that day and I found something inside of me.

The steps that I had taken to complete this goal were huge for me. Eating an elephant is not easy. I had completed the marathon by breaking it into tiny pieces and I discovered a new self-confidence inside of me that day, that I had not experienced before.

Running the streets of Paris that day changed me. I felt something shift inside me.

At the time of writing, there are 1.3 million recorded marathon finishers worldwide. Taking this as a data point for the number of people in the world who have run a marathon, we can determine the percentage of the population who have run a marathon. According to the US Census, the world population is approximately 7.928 billion. Therefore, only about 0.17% of the population has run a marathon and I was one of them. I was more tired than I had ever been in my life but inside I was so much stronger and empowered.

As Rob de Castello AO MBE said;

"We may run in circles ending up back where we started, but when we get back, we are not the same person we were."

I was not the same person. If I could achieve this, what else was I capable of?

> **Life Lesson**
>
> How do you eat an elephant or face a big challenge? One bite One step at a time.

CHAPTER 2

2010 New York Marathon # 1

> It is just as hard to get to the start line of a marathon as it is to get to the finish line.

Paris had been beautiful and running the marathon that day was a lot of fun and the effect on me was life-changing. I cried as I crossed that finish line. My sister passed me champagne that she had been carrying around all day and whilst I felt tired and emotional, I also had a different feeling in the pit of my stomach.

What else was I capable of achieving? If I achieve this with just 16 weeks of training what else could I do?

The ripple effect of running Paris was immediate. Returning to Sydney, many of the running group also wanted to run an international marathon. Ask any runner and they will say they sign up for the next race even before the muscle aches and pains have eased.

Within weeks, Coach Fi had entries for New York Marathon the following year. It was another sign; it was meant to be. Fi worked for one of the sponsors of the race and was able to work some magic. It is very hard to get an entry into most of the big marathons, but Fi knew someone who knew someone and she managed to get the whole running group an entry.

This is how running 12 marathons (to date) has happened for me, taking advantage of opportunities that have come along and just diving in without too much research. Not much of this journey was planned, so it was fun as I took the next step.

Before diving into the New York story, I hope that Paris may have inspired you just a little, so I want to explore how you might get started, maybe not with a marathon just yet, but by getting active. It is simple, just not always easy.

My passion is running, and the prime focus of this book is because it has been my journey, but it may not be your journey. I encourage you to find something that you think you will enjoy; it might be dancing, playing badminton or pickleball and yes, that is a real thing, as a friend of mine has recently discovered. Join a local group or find a meet-up group online.

Taking the first step is the hardest because few of us like being the new girl, not knowing anyone or wondering if we are any good.

However, after that first step, it does get easier and I hope this book will inspire you to take one step towards finding that passion.

If you decide running might be for you, buy specialised running shoes as opposed to any other sports shoes available. They are available at a reasonable price and will support your feet and ankles in ways that generic sports shoes will not. There is no need for fancy shoes until you see if you enjoy it, but we will revisit this topic as you get further into your running. Find a friend; running with a friend is added motivation and a lot more fun.

One way to do this is to find a local parkrun if you live in an area where there is one. Parkrun is a free weekly community run or walk and they are set up to overcome some of the challenges that being new to running throws up. You will quickly meet like-minded people if you have yet to find a friend who is keen to run with you. If this is not for you, there are many apps that you can download to your phone that will help you get from the "Couch to 5 km" in no time.

Having someone to hold me accountable has been a key to both my running success and achieving goals at work. Meeting my running buddy at 5.30 am means I have to show up. Imagine if they were at the meeting point and I was still sleeping! I can honestly say I have never let a running buddy down at that time of the day and I know for sure I would have let myself down at that time of the day many times. I love my sleep. An accountability colleague or mentor at work is just as important to keep you on track and focused on career goals or building your business. Knowing that someone has your back and that you have to explain why you have not done what you said you would do sure makes you do it!

These are all simple ways to get started with running. All you have to do is lace up your shoes, get out there and run. The harder part is sticking to it, but I found that when I had decided to do an event like the New York Marathon, I had friends who would run it with me and for me, that is a big part of why I love to run.

My running friends have become my closest friends and they hold me accountable. The running community is inclusive and accepting, making running a lot more fun. It is key to making it easier, but you still have to show up, be consistent with your training and choose not to let yourself down.

The New York Marathon is a big deal. It is one of the largest marathons in the world, with 50,000 runners and three million spectators. The New York Marathon starts on Staten Island. Then you cross the Verrazzano-Narrows Bridge into mostly-flat Brooklyn, where for the next 19 km, you pass through Bay Ridge, Sunset Park, Park Slope, Fort Greene, Bedford-Stuyvesant and Williamsburg. The course then enters Queens by crossing the Pulaski Bridge, the race's mid-point.

After a short time in Queens, the race crosses the Queensboro Bridge at 23 km and then enters Manhattan, where we run north on First Avenue for 4.8 km. Runners cross the Willis Avenue Bridge, where we enter the Bronx. The course then re-enters Manhattan via the Madison Avenue Bridge for the final 10 km. After running through Harlem, there is a slight uphill section along Fifth Avenue before it flattens out and runs parallel to Central Park. The course then enters Central Park around the 38 km mark, passes Columbus Circle and re-enters Central Park for the finish line.

Before all of that, however, comes the training. The training schedule was circulated and I again put every session into my electronic calendar. We ran four times a week. Intervals at the oval continued with the fast short sessions that have always challenged me and Fi threw in some hill training just to be sure we would be ready.

Long runs on Saturday mornings were mapped out and circulated by Jerry, one of the running group members who was also going to run the New York Marathon. Meeting early every Saturday morning became a regular thing and we did it for years to follow, even when there was no event to train for. It became a way to catch up with friends socially and went way beyond the running. Another ripple effect of running!

We would set off at the same time every week, but with varying ages and fitness levels, we would run at our own pace. We named ourselves KTP (Keep the Pace), which gave us an identity and a bond.

Down the track, we even designed a logo and printed shirts with the name on them. It was just a bit of fun. Coffee and breakfast, which sometimes turned into lunch when the runs were long, were a central part of the training.

Discussion on which shoes, which socks and how to manage the ever-growing injuries we were all experiencing were normal. As the group trained together, it somehow became a little easier, even though the runs got harder and fatigue was very much part of everyday life.

The eight runners going to New York consisted of a group of us who had started running together, that cold winter evening back in 2007. Our running group was growing, with more partners joining us; running and supporting. This diverse mix of humans that had formed from running that first 9 km was aged from 30 to 60+ and we were all aiming for the same finish line. From all walks of life and all with unique experiences, we trained together for the 2010 New York Marathon.

Another significant part of the training schedule for a marathon is managing your injuries, so you at least get to the start line. It is just as hard to get to the start line of a marathon as the finish line and quite possibly one of the hardest parts of running a marathon. I added a few more members to my support team to ensure I got to the start line with minimal injuries.

The first was a great physiotherapist who is also a great runner. Mark Green from The Body Mechanic became an integral part of my support team over the following years and with his help, I was able to get to the start line of every marathon, even when I was injured. Mark also has specialist online running programs that can be found at The Body Mechanic Locker Room. They are a great place to get your running plan from if you do not have one, as they are designed for all types of running events and I would go online to use these plans in later marathons. The plans he designs are not just about running. Mark focuses on injury prevention and builds in a lot of strength work that (if you do them properly) will help get you to that start line.

I also added an awesome remedial massage therapist who found knots in my muscles that I had no idea existed. The remedial massage became part of my regular schedule and was booked for every two weeks during training. It was not an hour of relaxation and meditation. It was an hour of brutal massage, to smooth out the increasing muscle aches and pains. It became a key component of future training and completing the following marathons.

My life was getting increasingly busy, so I fitted the massages in during my lunch hour. I had learned many years previously, whilst running my business from home, that the nooks and crannies you fill with worthwhile activities help create success. Running a marathon was no different.

While training for the Paris Marathon, I had a major knee issue. It was early in the training as my body adjusted to running the long distances it had not experienced before. As you embark on following new passions, some people will try to throw you off course with their negative comments and this knee pain gave cause for some negativity to be thrown at me. *"Running is bad for your knees"* was a common statement thrown at me, but I know that when I set big goals, big hurdles arise to test me and see how committed I really am. This was no different.

I had paid for the flights and nothing was going to stop me from running around the beautiful streets of Paris. Good advice, therapy and maybe a cortisone shot in my knee got me there, but it was just the first of many hurdles to challenge my marathon running.

I got to the start line of the 2010 New York Marathon relatively injury-free this time, thanks to the regular massages, but others in the New York group managed multiple issues. One of the running group had a stress fracture in his foot and had spent much of his training wearing a boot, which only came off days before the race. With little training completed and no long runs, the mind games began before the start line.

Even when you have completed all the training, you spend a lot of time questioning your ability to cross the finish line. It is a much harder battle mentally and physically when this has been compromised through illness or injury. Not deterred, he would give it a go and line up on that cold morning in November with the rest of us.

We were a group of eight mates running a marathon.

Heading to New York was immense fun. A ripple effect of entering the marathon was travelling to this amazing city with friends. Sharing the experience with others made it far more exciting. Once more, we headed to the expo, which was like a running shop on steroids. We spent most of the day there looking at gear, trying on gear and breaking the golden rule again of not wearing anything new on race day.

New gear not seen in Australia, new socks with the promise of no blisters and 2010 New York Marathon merchandise that we just had to have. A day spent shopping and exploring Macy's was probably not the best preparation for race day, but we were all on such a high.

Pre-race preparation involves much more organising when you are away from home. You need to purchase breakfast items that you tried and tested to eliminate any unwanted stomach issues, other than those that cannot be controlled by nerves. Ensuring you have enough food for fuel during the race and drinking enough fluid the day before takes some planning. You must be well-hydrated before the race, so I drank masses of water with electrolyte tablets and spent much of the day shopping, looking for toilets. But I think one of the most important elements is carbohydrate (or carb) loading.

With so many theories about how to do this, when to start and what to eat, I can only say that you do what feels right for you. I started "carb" loading five days before. Any excuse to eat? In New York, they had a pasta party the night before the marathon and we all went to the conference centre to join in the fun. There were thousands of competitors there and the atmosphere was electric. Fueled up on carbs, we were ready, training complete and well-hydrated.

Things then fell apart for one of the KTP group, Peita.

This was not Peita's first marathon. She had run the Sydney Marathon a year before and was determined not to let her finicky Anterior Cruciate Ligament (ACL) tendon impact the race as it did in Sydney. So armed with a physiotherapist, she incorporated more Pilates and swimming into her training and with plenty of cortisone injections in the lead-up to the event, she was ready.

As we queued for the pasta party, Peita was directed to a different line, selecting from a different buffet table from the rest of the group. It appeared inconsequential at the time as we re-joined at a table together and excitedly exchanged suggestions and pain points for the following day.

Sometime in the middle of the night, Peita woke with stomach pains and spent the rest of the night in the bathroom — very, very unwell. She says her saving grace was that she could open the bathroom window just a crack and get some fresh (but cold!!) November New York air. She called her parents back in Australia, seeking advice to stop her gastroenteritis. Still, their advice was repeatedly that she couldn't run because she was dehydrated, weak and exhausted.

Peita's husband, Adrian, made a post-midnight dash to a pharmacy (thank you, New York City, for your round-the-clock shopping), but the pharmacist was unwilling to suggest anything that would help. Peita was still determined to run until some wise words from her father hit home. "If you are sick (or worse) during the race, no cab driver will accept your fare and you will have to walk more than a marathon covered in muck back to the hotel." So, very reluctantly and feeling hugely devastated, she conceded. From behind the bathroom door, Peita asked Adrian to wish the team good luck as he headed downstairs at 4 am.

Peita watched the race on the TV, hoping for a glimpse of someone from our group and waited for Team KTP to come back to the hotel. She then listened to stories of glory and pain as the group recounted their race with their shiny medals proudly displayed.

After Googling "New York Marathon Pasta Party," she found hundreds of posts about food poisoning and assumed that had been her "sliding door" moment, she went one way to the uncooked chicken and the team went the other, everyone unaware of how that decision would unfold over the following 12 hours. Having not made it to the start line and being too unwell to cancel her registration before the event officially started, Peita is now unable to enter the New York Marathon again, with a black mark next to her name.

Now only seven of us lined up on that cold winter's morning. It was a very early start, as you must cross the Verrazzano-Narrows Bridge before they close it so that the runners can come back across it, during the race. We had all come prepared with old warm clothing that could be discarded at the start line and donated to charity. The final nervous 'wees' were done and we were in the corral waiting to start. Then, standing there in the cold waiting, I had another "sign" that had a massive impact on me.

As clothes were discarded, I saw that the girl next to me was wearing an old London Marathon running jacket and I started up a conversation with her about the Marathon. She was discarding the jacket as she had run that marathon a few years back and she no longer needed it and she offered it to me. To me, it was a sign that one day I might get the chance to run the streets of London as Nigel had. I took the jacket and tied it around my waist. I ran the entire New York Marathon with it.

The race was magnificent. Competing in a marathon is not really a race because I cannot win. However, I am competing against myself, so maybe I can call it a race.

An entire book would not be enough to describe the mixed emotions you feel running the streets of New York, supported by three million people cheering for you and shouting, *"You've got this,"* as you run past. I will try to give you a taste because I would love you to set a big goal and run a big marathon one day. It will change you.

Chad, my husband, now a fully trained member of my support crew, positioned himself in various spots around the city. The boost I got from seeing his face and silly hat as I turned a corner, lifted me mentally every time I saw him. The banner from Paris was on display again and we had added all of the group's names to it, so we could all see it as we ran past Chad.

I was so excited every time I saw him and forgot the fatigue and pain for a few minutes. The cheering crowds were on every corner as I tried to take it all in. They were so loud. We crossed numerous bridges, running quietly through the Jewish quarter where life continued as normal and then we ran into the Bronx. I lost Helen in a toilet queue along the way, so I ran the last marathon alone. My running watch ran out of battery at some point, so I had no idea what pace I was running and strangely enough, that was very liberating. I stopped worrying about what time I might do and just drank in the atmosphere. As I turned that last corner back into Central Park, with the finish line in sight, I was on a runners' high and knew this would not be my last marathon alone.

I finished the 2010 New York Marathon in a time of 4:38:39 hours. This was much quicker than I had run Paris in, as that had a five at the beginning. It just goes to show that consistently checking a running watch does not make me run any faster.

Eight of us had started and eight finished. The post-race celebration traditions that had started in Paris continued in New York with Billy Cart French champagne and chips. Lots of them!

Conversations about the next marathon went late into the evening and the idea of running five marathons in five years began to grow in my head.

With two already completed, I began to set a new goal.

You can train to run the marathon distance, but race day often has its own ideas, as I was later to experience. Peita is one of the strongest women I know who has been dealt some tough cards. We all have to find ways to bounce back from disappointments of goals set and not achieved. Peita is not a quitter and I know she will one day find a way to fulfil her dream of completing a New York Marathon.

The Paris Marathon had changed me and the New York Marathon changed Peita.

> Life Lesson
>
> Find an accountability coach.

CHAPTER THREE

2011 Berlin Marathon

> Suddenly, without realising it,
> I had labelled myself
> a runner and I believed it.

Today I headed out for a run for no real reason other than just to run; it was much like any other day. The Berlin Marathon is months away, so it is much too early to start a serious training schedule. Today I run just because I like to run and I enjoy the journey.

As I head down my favourite track, an unknown runner is waiting at the kerb, for a red traffic light to change. She asks me if I am training for anything special. My answer is simple, "No, just out for a run. How about you?"

She seems keen to chat and she readily shares with me her training plan for the upcoming event. She has a 10 km race just a few months away and her excitement reminds me of how I felt just a few years ago. I wish her well and she is on her way as the light turns green.

I continue my run, looking out over Sydney Harbour and heading down the Fairlight Track towards Manly. I think back to four years ago, when I was training for the 9 km run in the Sydney Running Festival and how big a goal that had been for me at the time – three months of training, sticking religiously to the training plan, increasing the distances a little each week, stretching, resting, watching what I ate and tapering. (We will return to what tapering is later.) There had been so much to think about as I prepared for that first race.

How quickly I had forgotten what it takes to run your first race and how much effort you put into it. Two marathons later, I had forgotten how important and daunting that goal had been to me then. The unknown runner that morning at the traffic lights was in the same headspace I had been, training for her significant milestone and one that if she is lucky like I was, will define her.

I look back now and I did not think I could run 9 km at the age of 47. My thoughts consume me as I continue on the stunning track that overlooks Sydney Harbour and I am disappointed in myself that I was not more supportive of the unknown runner that morning. I was beginning to take running for granted and could have encouraged her more.

As I reach the beach at Manly with 7 km under my feet, I have hardly thought about running. I can run this distance in my sleep now, a distance I had once thought impossible – and when I started, it was!

Suddenly without realising it, I had labelled myself a runner for the first time and I believed it. I was thinking back to not so long ago and when I was training for that first event, nervous and excited, I had never seen myself as a runner. I did now.

Jogging was the word many used for what I did, but today, I believed in myself as a runner, in my fancy running shoes and running socks.

I have now taken the time to get fitted at a running store for runners that suit my feet and running style. I ran on a treadmill in different shoes to see which would be best for me as they assessed my running gait; it was worth the extra money (in the "long run") as it saves on injuries and costly visits to the physiotherapist. More importantly, it allows me to keep running.

My brand of shoes has changed several times over the years as technology advances and my running style has also changed. It is a constant work in progress and a great excuse to go shopping! Shoes also have an expiry date. My rule of thumb, not based on any science, is to buy a new pair of shoes at the start of training for a new marathon.

During the training for a marathon, I run over 800 km. The cushioning wears down on the shoes and they will not support you as well as they once did. I let them retire at the end of each marathon. That is what I tell my husband anyway.

I have also been known to have two pairs of shoes on the go simultaneously. This way, there is more cushioning left in them by the time I get to the race. I never want to break in a new pair of shoes just before a major event, as that might cause blisters.

Shoes are the most essential part of running, but socks come a close second.

Socks. We have talked about socks on many a run and I have spent lots of money on socks. Helen's feet have been a constant topic on many long runs, but what goes on a run, stays on a run. She has tried nearly every running sock on the market: thick, thin, no-blisters, short socks and no-show ones – bamboo and lambswool.

The pain of blisters in a marathon is real and you want to do everything you can to avoid it, even if it involves wrapping lambswool around every toe. Getting the shoe and sock combination correct is a game changer. It only took me a few marathons, numerous brands of shoes and socks and more than a few Band-Aids.

It does take time to find the perfect combination of shoes and socks and I strongly recommend that you take the time to get professional advice on this – the shoes, at least.

What a difference it has made running a few steps, one after the other, completing a few running events and proudly displaying a few medals on my dresser at home.

I hope that I never take running for granted. I am privileged to have the freedom to run where I live. I feel safe when I run and I remind myself to enjoy the short runs and the long ones, the great runs, the not-so-great runs and even the tough interval training at the oval!

If I am honest, the 2011 Berlin Marathon is a means to an end – I would not have chosen it. It chose me. The opportunity to travel around the world with friends again and run another marathon with them was all part of my motivation. So, when a few of the running group decided the Berlin Marathon might be fun, I decided it might be part of a bigger goal.

The Abbott World Marathon Majors started as a series of five marathons worldwide – New York, Berlin, London, Boston and Chicago. It is now six, with Tokyo added in 2013, but when I planted the seed in my head, it was five. Very few runners manage to complete the series; to date, it is around 7,000 people worldwide and I had no idea at the time if it was at all possible. Learning about myself I knew that focusing on a big goal was very motivating and I had nothing to lose by trying. New York was done, so I had one ticked off and if I could run through the Brandenburg Gate in Berlin, I could tick off number two.

The Berlin Marathon entries were in and I started to dream just a little bigger.

When I joined a direct selling business in the UK, it was never a big career decision. It was a career break from teaching, giving me something to do whilst allowing me to be at home more and raise my children. I found juggling a full-time teaching job with no flexibility back then, negatively impacted them and I decided to take one year off, get them settled and then return to the teaching profession that I had studied hard to achieve.

Simply saying "*yes*" to starting a small business from home was another of those life-changing moments; I just did not know it at the time. I had no idea how to run a business, but a simple "yes" to the idea and I started to learn and within a few years, I was running a thriving business. This business was the one that gave me and my family the opportunity, to move to Australia.

Much like, "How do you eat an elephant?" that I had learned from Ann, not waiting for all of the traffic lights to be on green before moving forward was another big lesson I had learned in this business. So often, we wait for all the conditions to be correct to know precisely how we will do something before we take the first step forward with an idea, a passion project or a new goal.

When you drive down a motorway, do you wait for all the lights on the road ahead to be green? Not usually. We move forward on the green light, wait on the amber and stop (hopefully) for the red light.

Rarely are all of the conditions aligned perfectly with what we want to do, which can prevent us from even trying or taking that first step.

I had yet to learn how to run a business, but I started, got some training and made lots of mistakes and as I progressed, red lights turned to amber ones and back to green and often back to red again. That business opened many doors for me that I had never even dreamed possible, including the move to Australia and a life-long career in the direct selling industry.

If I had waited to feel confident about running a business and knowing what to do (with all the green traffic lights), I would never have started the business and I would have allowed fear to be my red traffic light. It is rarely smooth sailing all the way and using a traffic light system to navigate the hurdles helped me back then as it did now as I set new goals for myself in running.

Running marathons and setting this huge goal to complete the Abbott World Marathon Majors was similar. Just saying "yes" to the first event and overcoming that fear led to my first half marathon, then that first marathon in Paris and the second in New York. Now I am training for number three in Berlin and feeling quietly confident.

"I've got this," much like the crowd had shouted as I ran the streets of New York.

Starting anything new has an impact on other parts of your life, as I was learning once again. Rarely does everything line up at one time and it is ok to drop a few balls or stop at a few red traffic lights along the way, as long as you keep moving in the direction of the big goal.

Running was getting serious for me now and I was beginning to learn that I am a better human when I run. I am also nicer to live with (so my family tell me)! Running has helped me learn about myself and to understand what motivates and drives me. Running became an integral part of my life as I started to fit it into my work and home routines. Not needing to be done in a gym or at a particular time made it easy to run in the nooks and crannies of any spare time that I did have. It was hard fitting life in with teenagers turning into adults, a busy job that involved a lot of travel and if I was lucky, a social life.

I started running in different cities across Australia and other countries before my workday began. Running in cities and towns at dawn before they wake, has been another lovely ripple effect for me and one that, to this day, gives me a sense of awe and calm before my busy day begins. I have seen breathtaking sunrises that I would have missed had I been sleeping and experienced stillness in streets that have truly grounded me.

One such experience was running in the deserted streets of Christchurch New Zealand at 6.00 am before a meeting. It was eerie and confronting after the massive earthquake of 2010. I tried to imagine what it must have been like for the local people that day and wondered what terror they must have felt. I remember so vividly seeing an installation in the middle of the square that morning as I ran – 185 empty chairs that had all been painted white. They were all different – an old armchair, an office stool and a baby seat were just three chairs I saw that day, each one representing a life lost in that terrible disaster.

Running up a mountain trail to see the sunrise over Salt Lake City in Utah was a more uplifting experience. Marie, a work colleague and I left our hotel at 4.00 am to fit in a long run before work. We were both training for running events and nothing was going to stand in the way of us achieving our goals. We ran for a couple of hours; we chatted as we climbed the trail and stood watching the day dawn. We ran back to the hotel, showered quickly, grabbed a coffee and started work.

I have had similar experiences running in Hong Kong, Kuala Lumpur and other cities worldwide, including my hometown of Sydney. Running around the quiet streets of Sydney early one Sunday morning after the Sydney Gay and Lesbian Mardi Gras with streamers everywhere, street cleaners are out and the many partygoers who have forgotten to go home, litter the pavements.

When I am out early running, I see another side of a city before it wakes, before the crowds arrive. It has become just one of the many things I love about running. I would never have experienced these precious moments if I had not packed my shoes, set the alarm and carved out time for myself on these busy days. Filling the nooks and crannies or sacrificing a few minutes on the pillow has never been a disappointment. There is no such thing as a bad run, only the run you never did.

While training for the Berlin Marathon, life got messy for me on the job front. I found myself redundant, looking for a new job and as the primary income earner of the family, I was stressed. Losing your job shatters your confidence and that familiar fear in the pit of my stomach returned.

This was the first time I had been made redundant and I had to find a way to overcome the paralysing feeling it gave me. I was well and truly at a red light with no green lights in sight and I knew I had to change the colour. I returned to the feeling of crossing the finish line of the 2009 Paris Marathon when I believed I was capable of anything.

I felt empowered at that moment; the sense of achievement of completing the marathon distance was one I had never dared to dream possible. Crossing that finish line empowered me and I knew I could handle this situation, overcome the fear and find a new job that fulfilled me. Drawing on this moved my thinking to an amber traffic light.

The job redundancy had happened for a reason and maybe it was another "sign" I needed to pay attention to, but I needed a plan. Looking for a new job takes commitment and consistency, much like running a marathon and I decided to design a training schedule for finding a new job.

I wrote my "job finding plan" and diarised what I would do every day in my electronic calendar, alongside the Berlin Marathon training plan. I had to commit to it and be consistent with daily job-finding activities, just like when I trained for a marathon.

Training for the 2011 Berlin Marathon and finding a new job began in earnest. Running most days kept my mental health on track, allowing me to focus on the job-finding plan. Clearing my head as I pounded the streets day after day provided me with the mental clarity I needed as I planned the job task for that day to secure my next role. Running and the discipline of a marathon-training schedule energised me and made me more efficient with both goals.

Instead of spiralling out of control into a blubbering mess in front of the TV with a wine in my hand, I had this under control (most of the time). The mental toughness I had developed from running marathons was paying dividends and was showing up in other parts of my life I had never imagined possible. But even I was not prepared for the next ripple.

Interviewing for a role that I really wanted in an industry that I was not qualified for, I found myself chatting about marathon running with Mark, the Chair of the Board. Often now, I found that running had given me an interesting topic to talk about at networking events and my passion was evident. It is easy to chat about something you love doing and everyone usually has an opinion about running or runners. Either they love it or hate it; they used to run but gave up due to bad knees, or they were cyclists and did not understand why runners run when they could use two wheels.

So often in these conversations, the question about marathon finishing times came up. For some reason that I still do not understand, once someone knows that you ran a marathon, they want to know what time you ran it! It makes me smile.

Most people have no idea how far the marathon is, or what a good or bad time is and to be honest, I am puzzled as to why they care so much or why they ask. It is not a race. You cannot win (unless you are an elite runner). You are ecstatic just to cross the finish line, put the medal around your neck, drink Billy Cart champagne and eat chips (or maybe that is just me).

Most people have no idea what constitutes a good time, which I do understand because unless you are an elite athlete, the only good time is when you cross the finish line. For me, I am happy, sometimes surprised, to finish; whatever time it is, it is great and I forget it within days unless I write it down!

We call it a race, but in an international marathon of 50,000 runners, there are generally only four winners: male, female, male wheelchair and female wheelchair. The rest of us are all winners in our own way.

Back to Mark, the Chair of the Board, interviewing me. Sitting in an imposing room, in front of the interviewing panel for a role that I had done a lot of preparation for, really wanted and was not qualified for, I found myself chatting to Mark about running marathons. This was not going according to the plan I had prepared. Side-tracked in the interview, I relaxed and decided (in my head) that I had little hope of getting the role anyway and would enjoy the process.

I knew that green lights eventually lead to more green lights; it just might take time. Nailing an interview takes training, so I settled in and decided this was a training interview, not the main event. I was good at training.

A few days later, the call came and nobody was more surprised than me to be offered the role. It took my breath away. A million things were going on in my head and of the many things I could have and should have said, all I could say to Mark was, "Why me?"

Mark was laughing and I knew we would work well together. He explained that having run marathons himself, he knew what it took to cross a finish line after 42.195 km: passion, dedication, commitment and stamina. These were the qualities they needed in the new CEO. More than a ripple effect, that was a tidal wave for me that day.

As with many international marathons, the 2011 Berlin Marathon had a friendship run the day before the main event. The day before the marathon, a gentle 5 km run is good preparation and fun. It helps to calm the nerves, overcome the jet lag and ensure you have your running gear. (We will talk more about running gear in a later chapter.)

I am not sure why we decided to fly the Aussie flag at this one, to dress up and run with a blow-up kangaroo, but we did. We had to take a train to get to the friendship run and carrying a blow-up kangaroo made a few people stare. We arrived at the start, dressed in Australian t-shirts and temporary Aussie tattoos stuck to our arms and cheeks. There was music and dancing and the crowd loved our Skippy, a common name for a kangaroo down under. We were not the only ones to have the idea to dress up, with runners from all over the world uniting, dressing in national attire and breaking down barriers to run the streets of Berlin. It was so much fun.

With the expo visited and racing bibs collected, we were ready to run the marathon the next day.

My marathon that day was uneventful, which is a good thing, trust me. I was not to be so lucky in future marathons. Berlin is famous for being fast and flat. For me, running through the streets of this once-divided city was truly amazing and surreal. The Berlin Wall had divided the city and marathon events before 1990 were limited to West Berlin only. On 30 September 1990, athletes ran through the Brandenburg Gate for the first time and since then, the course has covered both halves of the unified city.

The course starts in the Tiergarten, Berlin's popular inner-city park and Jerry, our amazing map planner for our local runs, remembers the *Highlander*-type approach to the start, through the trees in the Tiergarten, as people popped up from every direction. Helen remembers them playing *The Ride of the Valkyries* as we crossed the start line. It was very inspiring and memorable.

Four of the KTP running group started the race; one stopped for a massage, but maybe he should remain anonymous and all four of us finished. I remember little of the run that day. I just enjoyed it. I crossed the finish line in a time of 4:36:34 hours, quicker than I had run Paris and New York Marathon, but it was a time I would go on to improve upon even more in the Chicago Marathon two years later.

My hero that day was Paula Radcliff, a UK long-distance runner who I had been following with interest and had a bit of a girl crush on. Paula returned to run the 2011 Berlin Marathon after multiple injuries and the birth of her second child. She had held the world marathon record for years at 2:15:25 hours (more than half as fast as my time that day). Paula came third that day with a time of 2:23:46 hours and qualified for the 2012 London Olympics.

I am not an elite athlete, but what other sports are there where a mere mortal runner like me can compete in the same race, on the same day, with true legends like her?

Putting into perspective the question so many ask about your finishing time, the female winner that day was Florence Kiplagat, from Kenya. She crossed the finish line in a time of 2:19:44 hours, which made her the ninth fastest woman of all time. This marathon course is fast and in 2018 Eliud Kipchoge ran 2:01:39 hours and held the marathon record for the course.

Kipchoge, Kenya's long-distance master, made history in the 2022 Berlin Marathon when he ran 02:01:09 hours, smashing his marathon world record by 30 seconds. I was not fast, but I was consistent and I was determined. This had held me in good stead with my career and was now paying dividends in my running.

It was such an honour that day to run through the Brandenburg Gate and cross the finish line of the 2011 Berlin Marathon. The celebrations continued well into the night.

> **Life Lesson**
>
> Just say "yes" and do not wait for all of the traffic lights to be on green, they never are.

CHAPTER 4

2012 London Marathon

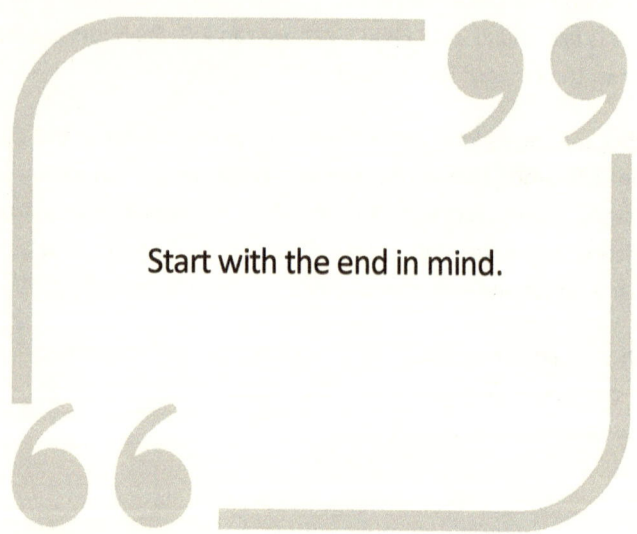

Start with the end in mind.

Running the London Marathon was always going to happen, once I started running marathons.

"Start with the end in mind" is another mantra I use often, both at work and in my running. When I can see in my mind how the completed project or race is going to look and feel it gives me great focus.

My brother Nigel had run the 2002 London Marathon and that was one of the many things that inspired me to start running. This and the London Marathon jacket that I still own, given to me by an unknown runner at the start of the 2010 New York Marathon, were both "signs" that I had to run it. I had seen myself running this race many years previously and now, it would be my number three in the Abbott World Marathon Majors.

Starting with the end in mind, I will give you a taste of what it is like to cross the finish line of this iconic race before returning to the start of the 2012 London Marathon.

Heading towards Buckingham Palace, I could smell success. I looked around at all the people on the side of the road, trying to soak it all in and wondering where Chad (my husband) and daughter Shelby were. I knew Chad was in the crowd somewhere, wearing his now renowned silly hat that I could usually spot from afar and it always lifted my spirits.

Buckingham Palace was now on my left as I turned into The Mall and I could see the finish line of the 2012 London Marathon. It took all my mental and physical strength to run those final few metres. The end was in sight. A marathon is 42.195 km and I only had 0.195 km to go.

As I ran across the timing mat under the finish line archway, I pressed stop on my watch – 4:21:16 hours. A personal best. My feelings at that moment were so mixed:

> *Relief: I had thought in the last few miles I may not make it this time.*
>
> *Fatigue: I was exhausted with nothing left in the tank.*
>
> *Emotional: Sad because I wished Helen was there to share the achievement.*

Emotional: Joyful at making the last 0.195 km and wearing the medal around my neck.

Tearful: I was so happy my stomach was churning with excitement

The finishing stretch of the London Marathon before Buckingham Palace is nothing short of spectacular – it is breathtaking. I was spent, with nothing left in the tank, running alongside the River Thames along the Victoria Embankment at about the 35 km mark, but as it is measured in miles, I should say the 22-mile mark. I had gone out way too fast in the first half of the marathon, caught up in the excitement of it all, without Helen to pace me.

I thought I could fly (well, I thought I could run faster than I can) and one thing Coach Fi had tried to teach me was to run the race with a negative split; that means running the first half slower than the second half, leaving enough fuel in the tank for the finish line. I had not listened and I was paying for it now. I was closer to giving up than I had ever been.

Rounding the corner at Westminster Bridge, the crowds were electric, the cheers deafening and there was no way I was walking now. They lifted my morale; my spirit and my energy lifted. It was because of this atmosphere in those final moments that I made it to the end. At this point in the London Marathon, my mental training had taken over. I had nothing left in the physical tank but mentally I was not going to give up. I was too close to the finish line.

A well-known ultra-runner Michael D'Aulerio said, *"Your body doesn't give up on race day, it's your mind that has the final say."* Your mind is the most powerful tool you have in your training schedule. I had been training myself for years to overcome the distance and now I needed it the most. It had to carry me through the last mile. My mind was strong and it did not let me down

Just after I had crossed the finishing line and proudly wearing my medal, I found Jerry. The photo of him and me in the finishing area is hilarious. Jerry is over 1.8m tall. I am just a little over 1.5m. He towered above me. We wore the 2012 London Marathon finisher medal around our necks and had space blankets to keep us warm. I was crying; the emotion of the day came flooding out. Poor Jerry!

It had been a long race. Getting to the start line of any marathon is hard and London was no different. It is difficult to even get an entry into this race; some say impossible. My niece has entered the lottery numerous times and has yet to get a place.

Once again, Coach Fi had worked her magic with her network. I will forever be grateful to Fi for her help in securing these entries and her pragmatic approach to training.

Only two starters from KTP this time, as life starts to get in the way for some of the running group. For me, it had been mentally tough getting to this start line, as it was going to be the first marathon I had run without Helen and the first training I had completed on my own. Jerry, a much faster runner than me and with much longer legs, as the photos of that day demonstrate, would run ahead of me, keeping his own pace. I would run alone, amongst millions of other runners.

Logistically it was also hard to get to the start line of the London Marathon. Jerry and I had set off together for the start line in Blackheath, Greenwich just a few hours earlier, ready to take on the 26.2-mile challenge, the imperial distance of a marathon. He had stood for hours in the portaloo queue with me. What a legend! The toilet queues at the start line of most marathons are horrendously long, as every runner lines up with pre-race nerves. Sensing Helen was not around, I think Jerry did it to keep me or maybe both of us calm.

At the start of the marathon, we were directed into different corrals. So, we separated and headed off towards the Cutty Sark at mile six. It was magnificent. The atmosphere around Cutty Sark is electric on Marathon Day, as it is one of the most popular sections of the course for spectators.

From there, I remember running past The Shard, a spectacular building in the London landscape now, but in 2012 it was still under construction. It is here that you reach Tower Bridge and cross the River Thames from the south to the north side. It is the halfway point. A half marathon completed with only a half marathon left to go!

The London Marathon is unique because it is a huge charity event and many run it in fancy dress. It can be unnerving to be beaten by a runner in a rhino suit (yes, true story), but to be overtaken by a blue smurf is a memory I would rather forget.

Chad and Shelby were standing on Tower Bridge. I saw the hat first, so I knew where to look for them. Shelby, now working overseas, had just completed climbing Mount Kilimanjaro, the highest mountain in Africa, standing at 5,895 metres (19,341 feet). Drawing on her immense achievement helped to get me through the next few miles.

She had come all this way to cheer me on. I had to cross the finish line to make it worth her while and I had no idea at the time that we would run a marathon together in just a few years.

Apart from going out too fast, the London Marathon was nearly a textbook race for me. No chafing, which can be very painful after many hours of running, your running gear having rubbed your skin raw and I had managed to escape the blisters that had plagued me in other races. I had finally got the gear right.

Another essential running gear item is the sports bra, not just to look good but to feel good and prevent chafing. I am talking about the women runners now, but I understand that nipple chafing for men is real and I believe easily prevented by Band-Aids again. Ask David, Helen's husband!

You do not want your boobs bouncing around and I can tell you from personal experience chafing in this area must be avoided. The correct sports bra is not expensive; it just takes practice to find the right one. Running in different bra styles until you find the bra that works for you, is the only way I know how to get this right.

I know I like to pack the boobs down and squash them tight and secure, so I can run with as little movement or bounce as possible. The only disadvantage of this for me comes at the end of a marathon, when I find it impossible to get a good sports bra off, by myself. It is so tight and I am always so tired. Chad needs to be around to assist, but maybe that is oversharing.

The rest of the gear, leggings or shorts, a long or short sleeve top, is all personal preference. I have tried them all, from compression leggings that cling tight to your thighs and are said to speed recovery to wicking fabric – a fabric that breathes and supposedly stops you from smelling.

They are all great. I now have a cupboard full of running clothes and I love them all. The ripple effect of running is fuelling my shopping passion. I have a drawer for tops, bottoms, rain jackets and running underwear. When I travel, I love to visit a local running store and always buy something I have not seen before. It would be rude not to! But you do not need much to run; focus on the shoes and socks. The rest is just to feel the part.

I have said it many times, but running is my little secret to success, happiness and thriving through challenging times.

Another ripple effect of running in my forties and fifties has been reducing the dreaded menopausal symptoms. I indeed have no idea what menopause would have been like for me without running, but I do know that with running, the sleepless nights and insomnia that so many of my friends went through were very minimal for me. I was always so physically tired, sleep came quickly.

Recently I trained with a friend who was menopausal and on medication for insomnia. One month into marathon training and she reduced the tablets. Two months into training, she was not taking them at all.

Weight gain is another significant side effect of menopause and one many seem to take for granted. Training hard and focusing on a goal means you have to eat healthily. There is no point in training otherwise. It also means drinking less alcohol, which helps with weight control.

I have now added another member to my support team. Brenda Rogers is a Sydney-based healer and naturopath and the founder and CEO of Quintessence, a boutique wellness company grounded in solid, evidence-based nutrition, herbs, energetic healing and feminine-focused personal growth who has some great insights on menopause.

"In the West, we grow up with a deeply negative perspective on menopause. Before we even reach it, we have already decided it is something that we are going to completely ignore, hoping it will just roll over us like a wave we have ducked under," said Brenda.

If you are reading this book, then you are probably one of those rare people who has decided that you are going to embrace the freedom and opportunity that menopause offers. As Brenda says, *"Yes, it is a challenge. Yes, it can be a wild ride. But it can also lead you into the most empowering, liberating and passionate time of your life."*

One of Brenda's best recommendations is to be prepared. She recommends ensuring you are fit at 40 and ready at 45 when menopause typically begins. Make sure you are protecting your energy. Hormone disruption is virtually guaranteed and will not help your sleep, weight, moods or self-esteem if your adrenals are shot. And, like me, she is a great believer in having a posse of great support around you – your massage therapist, your kinesiologist, your running buddies, your women's circle and if you have not already, you will need both a great naturopath and a financial planner!

I firmly believe that I sailed through menopause with the help of running and Brenda. I eat better, sleep better and drink less wine. The feeling I get when I head out the front door, sunscreen, or beanie in hand lifts my spirit and keeps those kilos in check.

I hope that you feel inspired to find a way of being more active. It does not have to be running, but it needs to be something you are passionate about and makes you want to *"move mountains"* to achieve. Being active regularly takes time and commitment, so it must be an activity that you fall in love with. Try a few activities like I did and you will find your version of running. Start with the end in mind and see yourself achieving your goal, being more active, and feeling upbeat and energetic.

I am convinced you must keep moving to stay mentally and physically healthy.

In 2016, in its 35th year, the millionth runner crossed the finish line of the London Marathon. I was one of that number in 2012. To mark the *#oneinamillion* finishers of the London Marathon, every runner who had ever completed the race was offered the chance to buy a personalised t-shirt with the number of where they were placed in that million on it. I was the 835,740th of that million runners to cross the finish line and I have the t-shirt with *#835740* in my drawer for tops!

"Starting with the end in mind"; seeing in my mind how I want something to turn out gives me great direction and focus at work and in my running. I had seen myself crossing the finish line of this marathon in The Mall many years before I crossed it; as far back as when I had been given the London Marathon jacket back in New York and tied it around my waist. I had imagined it on many long runs.

I was now getting closer to completing the goal of running five marathons in five years. Finishing the 2012 London Marathon was my fourth marathon in four years. I had the end in mind. I was planning number five for 2013. And I was starting to believe that my new goal of completing the five Abbott World Marathon Majors, might just be possible with only Boston and Chicago Marathons left to complete.

The 2012 London Marathon was completed and I am happy to say it was epic. Post-race celebration traditions were in full force.

I would not be so lucky in 2013.

> **Life Lesson**
> Start with the end in mind, and let the journey take care of itself.

CHAPTER 5

2013 Boston Marathon #1

> The experience that day had to stand for something.

When people find out that I was there that day, that I was running the 2013 Boston Marathon, on the very day the bomb went off, that I was 700 metres from the finish line, the immediate reaction is fear. "Oh, my goodness! Were you ok?"

The 2013 Boston Marathon bombing was a domestic terrorist attack that occurred during the annual Boston Marathon on 15 April 2013. Two terrorists, brothers, planted two homemade pressure cooker bombs, which detonated 14 seconds and 210 yards (190 m) apart at

2:49 pm, near the marathon's finish line, killing three people and injuring hundreds of others, including 17 who lost limbs.

Helen and I were so lucky that day, we had no physical injuries. Seven hundred metres is actually a long way and we had two corners left to run before we reached the finish line, but that day, that experience, changed the direction of my life once again.

Coach Fi had been unable to work her magic with entries for the race this time, so I started to reach out to my network of friends and colleagues. They all knew about my passion for running marathons by now and I was hoping someone might know someone who could help me reach my goal.

The Boston Marathon is unique because to gain an entry, you have to achieve a qualifying time at a previous marathon. I was now 53 and would have needed a qualifying time of under 4:05:00 hours, which would never happen. Not even close, or so I thought!

I have yet to achieve that time, so I should not have been at the start line on that fateful day, but my network came through. It took some time and persistence, but I secured two spots in the 2013 Boston Marathon from a friend of a friend who knew someone!

I remember standing on the corner of a busy street in Sydney, having just finished a meeting, when I got the call, but I was so excited I could not wait until I got home. I called Helen immediately. The Boston Marathon is the Holy Grail for a runner. It is an iconic event in the running calendar.

Helen, now living in Melbourne, said yes instantly. This would mean I could complete my goal of running five marathons in five years and it was a step closer to completing the Abbott World Marathon Majors. With me living in NSW and Helen in Victoria, we completed the marathon training remotely this time. Still, we made it work by texting our completed runs and holding each other accountable. We could have done this by using Strava, a great running app that tracks all your runs, your pace and many other statistics but we kept it simple.

The Boston Marathon course starts 42.195 km outside of the city. Big yellow school buses, as you see on Sesame Street, take you out to the town of Hopkinton. We were on the school bus listening to "*It's a beautiful day*" by U2 on the radio. The nerves we had experienced at the start of other marathons were overtaken by sheer excitement about what we were about to do – run the Boston Marathon! We got off the bus and walked through the streets of Hopkinton, where every member of the village seemed to be out on their verandas waving and embracing the runners. I remember seeing the signs "Hopkinton, Welcomes the Runners" everywhere. I was so happy that day.

We lined up towards the back, with thousands of other runners, as this is where the slower runners start, allowing the faster ones to get going without too many slower ones causing congestion. They called us the "back of the pack runners."

Helen and I spent the next few hours running from Hopkinton, through many different suburbs, towards the finish line in Boston. Running through numerous suburbs, the streets were lined with cheering spectators all the way. Students from Wellesley College encourage runners with signs and cheers that keep your spirits up when the going gets tough. Chad and David, our husbands, had been at different spots on the course waving, cheering and holding the now-traditional race banner with our names on it.

My niece Steph made the banner in 2009 for the Paris Marathon out of an old cloth and a few pink Sharpies (marking pens). It was well travelled now. The banner has been to every marathon I have run and what had started with just the names of Helen and me on it grew, as the list of marathoners grew. It now has many names on it. We are going to need a bigger banner pretty soon! Steph went on to take up marathon running after living with us in Sydney for a few months and she completed her first one in 2016. The ripple effect of my running continues.

It was just before 3:00 pm on 15 April 2013 and we had completed 41.5 km. Nearly there. A marathon is 42.195 km, as I have mentioned a few times, but that final 0.195 km gets you across the finish line, achieving the goal and having the medal placed around your neck. Stopping any earlier is not completing the race or the goal, and that is why I always add the 0.195 km to the end of 42 km every time a marathon distance is mentioned.

It was a great run—so much fun. We were on fire and on track for a fabulous time (for us, anyway). We had run through the 35 km mark, which is usually a real mental barrier for us, but not today. The atmosphere was amazing and it carried us all the way. Only two corners left to run, two corners left until we reached the water, food, space blankets and our husbands cheering madly. It was less than five minutes to the finish line and the coveted 2013 Boston Marathon medal.

As we approached the last but one corner to turn onto Boylston Street, where we would see the finish line, the road, the view and the scene in front of us changed instantly. We saw a congestion of runners up ahead. We had no idea what was going on as we continued to run towards them.

A backup of runners sometimes can happen in a race, generally nearer the start, though, as the mass of excited runners leaves the start line. The course can sometimes be narrow for them all, but we had never seen a bottleneck so close to the finish line. Marathon runners are usually more spread out by now. We were, after all, classified as "back of the pack runners," runners who had not qualified for this prestigious event and were more likely to be slower than the qualifiers.

We got closer to the mass of runners. They were stopped. Not just running slowly. Runners not running with such a short distance to go and we had no idea why.

We stopped. We waited. We listened.

Had someone had a medical incident just up ahead? That was the chatter. We were sure we would be running again shortly. Again, an unfortunate but not uncommon occurrence for this distance is seeing a runner at the side of the road. The endurance needed to run 42.195 km can trigger hidden health issues, previously undiagnosed; hence it is always best to get checked medically before running such a distance. This was not the case today.

We paused our running watches; no one wants to add a stop time to their race time, especially at this stage in the marathon. We moaned; Helen was up for a P.B. (Personal Best). We chatted about this temporary pause and whether it would count towards the final time. Was it cheating to deduct the stoppage time?

It sounds so futile now, but by the time you have run this distance, fatigue is real and some of the brain cells do not work as well as you would like them to, if at all. We were just trying to keep each other in the right headspace as we stood still, waiting to start running again.

It was then that someone said, "There's been an explosion up ahead" but still, there was no panic. A simple use of words here made all the difference. No one seemed fazed by the word *explosion* but the questions started! Annoyance at first, frustrated at not knowing when we could complete the final 700 metres, start the running watch again and run the last two corners to cross the prestigious blue and yellow finish line we had seen yesterday. We always checked out the race's final stages before running so we could start with the end in mind.

Then, the word changed from explosion to **'bomb'** and the mood changed from annoyance to fear.

Twitter was relatively new at that time. The locals took to Twitter to find out what was going on. The bomb was at the finish line, where our two husbands were waiting for us. Real fear took hold of us.

This was quickly followed by cold and exhaustion as the adrenalin dropped. I had a jumper around my waist so that I could put that on. I took off my arm warmers, which I gave to Helen as she had thrown her jumper to David earlier in the race. To this day, I do not know why I did this; they would never keep her warm. My brain cells were not fully functioning!

Fear works in mysterious ways. I have little memory of what happened in the following minutes as we just stood and sat on the ground, unsure of the next step or even if we could take one. With our adrenaline dropping and a lack of fuel and warmth, we were beginning to fade fast.

Helen took a call from David, who said, "Sorry we cannot get to the finish line. We have no idea what is going on, but we cannot get near it to cheer you across the line." We knew why and were grateful, for once, that they were running late and were not at that line.

Then we saw large black SUVs everywhere, sirens blaring and helicopters overhead. It was chaos. The realisation that our race was run began to set in. We were not going to run anywhere anytime soon and we were not going to cross the finish line that day.

Phones with any battery power left were shared around, allowing runners to contact loved ones and let them know that they were okay. Fear set in and many started to panic as we all got cold, tired and hungry.

A marathon distance is designed with all of the support crew at the finish line, waiting with space blankets, water and food. No one plans for 5,000 runners to stop 700m before the end. It dawned on Helen and me quite quickly that if we did not move and get out of there soon, we too would need help. We would add to the chaos.

We had no idea what to do.

In some situations, you have to be brave enough to walk away, which is what we decided to do. We got up off the ground, turned around and walked back along the course we had just run. What was to have been our final victory kilometre was now our way out.

We were not as quick as we had been just minutes before, certainly not as light-hearted. We were despondent, disappointed, self-absorbed, shocked, angry and fearful as we walked away from the finish line. Our race was well and truly over. My goal to complete five marathons in five years and the Abbott World Marathon Majors was shattered in those minutes, but it was inconsequential. We knew lives would have been lost. We had no idea if there were more bombs likely to explode, so tired, cold and hangry (we hadn't eaten for hours), we just walked.

We walked for what seemed like ages, trying to navigate our way through the chaos to meet up with Chad and David. I was so cold. It was late on a spring day in Boston and my body was severely fatigued. The finish line space blankets we had worn in London and New York were nowhere to be found.

Local Bostonians were amazing. They came out of their houses with water, food and garbage bags—plastic garbage bags for us to make a hole in the top and pull over our heads. We knew what they were for now and they would keep us a little warmer. I pulled the black bag over my head. The arm warmers that Helen was wearing were useless and we were both cold. I did not care what I looked like.

As we walked, locals offered us extension cords to charge flat phones. They were strung out of the brownstone houses, enabling other walkers like us to call and reassure loved ones that they were safe. It was late in the day, Spring in the air, but the sun had gone down by 3.30 pm and along with it, so had our spirits. Bostonians still with no idea what had happened or what was to come. These small acts of kindness meant so much to us on that day.

Finally, we stopped walking and wearing that garbage bag to keep warm, I sat on the stoop of a stranger's brownstone house. The city was now in lockdown. As I sat there, shaken to the core, lost and feeling really cold now, I realised that this was not the only place where I had lost control over my path and its direction.

As I walked away from the goal that had meant so much to me, I suddenly realised it was also time to read the signs and walk away from my job back home. I turned to Helen and said, "I have to quit my job." There are many times in life when we stay in a role, stay in relationships that do not serve us and even though the signs are there, we do not act on them soon enough. It was time to act.

What I thought had been a dream role just two years earlier, was toxic and I knew that I could not change the toxicity in that organisation. It was destroying my confidence and self-esteem. If we had run each kilometre just a few seconds quicker, we would have been at the finishing line when the bomb went off. We were only five minutes away. As I faced what could have been a far more serious life-altering moment than it was, the effect rippled through me and I made life decisions at that moment that would significantly impact me in the future.

It was time to change direction in Boston and at work.

Chad and David found us. They had located us using Find my Friends on the iPhone. We walked back to the car that was parked so far away. I felt like I was walking another marathon, but we were all safe.

Chaos ensued, sirens were going off everywhere and I panicked about the kids back home. What would they think when they woke up in Sydney in just a few hours and heard what was, by now, international news? Hours in front, I called Shelby, who was still fast asleep and none too pleased to be woken up before dawn by her hysterical mother.

"When you hear the news on the TV, do not worry, we are all right." With no idea what her mum was blabbing about on the phone and not the best morning person, an explanation followed. Shelby sprang into action, letting friends, family and colleagues know, posting across social media so that they did not worry. It was then that the calls started coming from family in the UK and friends in Sydney. Everyone cared and was concerned.

The city was in complete lockdown and runners could not return to their hotels. Luckily Chad had made the hotel booking and what should have been a hotel in the city was a motel in the suburbs. We had given him grief about this just the day before. Now, we were so grateful. We got out of the city and headed for our motel. Starving, we popped into the ranch-type bar opposite the motel before showering and the events started appearing on the TV. As the enormity of the day unfolded on the screen, it slowly sank in.

The post-race rituals were abandoned. We had not reached the end. We had not finished. People were dead and maimed.

The media calls started shortly after. Helen and I were both high-profile women in leadership positions back home and the media wanted the scoop. Flattered and uplifted, we saw it as a way to get the information out. Helen and I agreed to talk to them. The next few hours were surreal.

Helen and I were standing outside the bar, on the street corner, as we spoke to the media in Australia, still in our running gear, frightened and feeling like frauds.

"What was it like?" they asked. "How loud was it? What was it like at the finish line? Tell us about the chaos."

Questions came, but we had no answers. Two corners from the end, thankfully, we had not heard the bomb. Two corners from the end, we had not seen anything! We were not hurt. We were all OK. We felt cheated out of the race finish line honours that we had trained months for. We had flown halfway around the world and we had not crossed the finish line. We had no medals placed around our necks. Talking about it seemed wrong.

It was wrong. We had nothing to say, nothing to add to the conversation. People had died. We had no idea how many at that time. We stopped talking to the media.

The days that followed saw us watch every bit of news coverage we could. With mixed emotions we watched safely from our New York hotel room, having left Boston in the early hours of the next morning, not wanting to be there, just in case there were more bombs. One of the bombers was still hiding somewhere in the streets of Boston.

We were the lucky ones, although we did not feel like it at the time.

Few event organisers plan for this type of crisis, but Boston handled it superbly. I cannot praise their crisis management plan highly enough. How do you care for hundreds of maimed runners and spectators, people displaced with a city in lockdown and a bomber on the run? Boston and the local Bostonians had it covered. The garbage bags and phone chargers were just two of the many amazing, respectful ways they helped us race day. In the days and weeks to follow, this respect and support continued, even for those not injured and not directly affected by the bomb.

We had only been slightly disadvantaged by not being able to complete a goal that we had set out to do four hours earlier, four months before. Event organisers offered online counselling if required and the finishing medal was sent to us in the mail, even though we had not crossed the finish line. Mine stayed in the packaging.

The experience that day had to stand for something and I could no longer accept the work situation that did not align with my values. I took action. In the aftermath of the 2013 Boston Marathon, I returned home to Sydney and I resigned.

Crossing the finish line of a marathon changes you forever and this one was no exception. I was stronger and more in control of my life than I had been for a while. I was taking steps to change the colour of traffic lights and re-invent myself once again.

The silver lining came in the months to come when the race organisers offered us an opportunity to return to Boston and run the 2014 Boston Marathon.

Life Lesson

Look for the signs, follow your intuition and take action.

Chapter Six

2013 Chicago Marathon

> You do not run a marathon to stop feeling or run away from a feeling. You run a marathon to feel 'something' and find 'something' inside yourself.

The 2013 Boston Marathon profoundly affected me and empowered me to *"find something inside myself,"* an inner strength I did not know I had. I changed the circumstances that were not serving me. I knew I was in the wrong role with the wrong culture and I was running away from taking control of it rather than facing it. Running Boston in 2013 changed that.

Resigning from your job may sound simple, but as the family's primary breadwinner and in my 50s, I knew I would have a big challenge ahead of me in finding a new role. As if that was not enough, we decided to stir things up a little more. It was a beautiful morning, I was out running thinking things through when I just knew it was the right time to sell the house, we had owned for over ten years. An interesting post-run conversation with my husband.

It was hard to walk away from a job that, just 24 months earlier, had been what I thought was my dream role, but it was slowly destroying my confidence from the inside out. It was unnerving to quit a job when I did not have a new one to go to and as the sole income earner, I was worried. We were also selling the house with no idea where to move. But none of it felt hard this time. When the decision feels right, it is not hard to make.

I learned on that day in Boston that leadership is knowing when it is time to pivot, re-create your own life and take action. That is exactly what I did on my return to Sydney.

Jobless and renting, I felt lighter and happier than I had for a while. I could breathe again and I started to re-focus but deep down in my heart, that little running voice began again and I knew I had to find a way to complete my running goal.

Completing five marathons in five years and the Abbott World Marathon Majors was still something I had to do and I only had a little time left that year, to do it.

During all this new chaos that I had created and with plenty to keep me busy, I entered the lottery for an entry into the 2013 Chicago Marathon. If I was not counting the 2013 Boston Marathon as a completed marathon, I needed another one for that year to stay on track with the five in five years goal. The Chicago Marathon is also part of the Abbott World Marathon Majors and completing it would complete the series if I then decided to count Boston. I had the 2013 medal to prove it, but it did not feel right. I had not completed it.

Those last 700 metres still needed to be run and they had offered us a place for next year, so that could work.

The Boston Marathon event organisers had decided that officially, even though we had not crossed the finish line, 2013 counted towards the Abbott World Marathon Majors. Receiving that Boston Marathon medal in the mail was nowhere near the same as having it put around your neck after crossing the coveted blue and yellow finish line. I still did not feel that I could count it. Not yet, anyway!

I was learning that the best things happen when you do all you can to achieve a goal, follow the signs and then let go of the outcome. If it was meant to be, I would get a place to run in the 2013 Chicago Marathon and I would complete the five in five.

A worthy goal will often present hurdles to jump over, just to see how committed you are to achieving it. I was committed and could jump, but I had no control over the lottery entry! I decided to let go of the outcome of the marathon and let fate take its course. I put my energy into what I did have control over – finding a new job and selling the house.

In case I got lucky with the entry and trusted my instinct, I stuck to the marathon-training schedule, while I packed up the house and started job hunting.

Some mornings it was hard to crawl out of bed before sunrise, but one of the many things running has taught me is that I might let myself down by not going for a run, but I will never let my running friends down. I will be at the meeting point in rain, hail or sunshine and we have had plenty of wet runs and hot runs.

I show up if I have arranged to meet someone for a run. It is accountability.

There is a sense of a common goal or purpose. It might be an event that we have entered or overcome a bad week at work and we all have those. Today was no different, a busy week of job hunting again and a restless night's sleep. I was not in the mood for an early run, but a girlfriend and I had arranged to meet at 7 am. It should have been just a regular training run through the beautiful city of Sydney, but it was so much more.

Meeting early, the conversation started with, "How was your week?"

"Pretty normal, long hours and a few late nights. You know the score!"

As so often happens, what was to be just a regular run can surprise you in the most inspirational ways. A great running friend of mine, Marie (and I am so lucky I have a few), told me years ago that your running friends become your closest friends, but until that morning, I had not fully understood what she meant.

Marie runs distances that I can only ever dream of doing, but in this case, she was referring to shared experiences and how they bond a friendship as you spend time pounding the streets. Sharing innermost thoughts as you run through the suburbs is not uncommon as you run out of TV shows to chat about and the weekly moan about the challenges of work and menopause has ended. We always stick to the unspoken rule of, *"What goes on a run, stays on the run."* Secrets shared on the run are not shared outside of the run.

My running partner this morning talked for two hours about her past, her upbringing, her family and some innermost secrets that she had not previously shared with anyone. What a privilege it was for me to know someone on this level, to earn their trust and have this depth of conversation. As I listened intently, I felt connected to something much bigger and far more important than just running.

How many times do we have shallow, meaningless conversations? Running is not unique, but the time spent on your feet, training, sometimes for hours, has allowed me to build deep connections and lasting friendships that I truly value. These connections, that span runs, distance, time and locations, have grounded me in Australia, the country I now call home. I have explored cities and neighbourhoods that I would never have seen and I have made lasting friendships by taking this time out for my physical and mental health.

It does not have to be running if running is not your thing, but it does have to be something physical to gain the benefits that I have experienced and you do need to be very passionate about it. I love yoga, cycling, spin classes and walking, but I am committed to running more profoundly. It does not matter what the goal is – it just matters that you show up, join in and have fun; well, most of the time anyway as we all know, sometimes it is just hard work.

Running has made me a better person. Sometimes I wish I had discovered the love of running before I was 47, as I am sure I would have had better marathon finishing times, seen more places and had more crazy adventures. It has helped me through some tough times, including the dreaded menopause and I am happy that I can still run in my sixties. I am grateful that I found my passion and hope you find yours.

I plan to keep running well into my eighties and I will not worry about my knees, hips, joints and other physical issues that await me because I would have gotten them at some stage anyway. The benefits of better-quality sleep, less hot flushes and managing my mental health that I have had from 15 years on my feet, far outweigh any potential physical issues down the track.

Listening to my running friend that day as her deep secrets were shared, I was a better person for that run. I was listening, engaged and open to different perspectives and ways of life and I felt better able to understand some issues around diversity and inclusion. There are moments in time that stay with you forever and this day, this run, was just one of many that I have had while out running.

I did get an entry into the 2013 Chicago Marathon. It was the sign that I had been waiting for. It was meant to be. I was so excited; I was back on track. I was going to run the beautiful city of Chicago and I had kept up the marathon training, so I knew I could finish. I was going to complete my goal.

The Abbott World Marathon Majors would be completed when I crossed the finish line in Chicago, as I decided the "sign" of getting an entry into the 2013 Chicago Marathon meant I could count the 2013 Boston Marathon as number four of the series. Counting Boston also meant that I would run my sixth marathon in five years, so my five-in-five goal would be ticked off.

October 2013 came upon me very quickly and by now, we had sold the house, packed up and moved into a rental property. I also had a new job to return to after the marathon.

Marathon day was fabulous. The events in Boston taught me to dig deep and to be prepared for the fact that anything can (and does) happen on race day. The training schedule only gets you to the start line. I now knew that anything might occur during the race before I reached the finish line and that crossing it was a bonus. I was ready.

The Chicago Marathon is unique, with the start and finish lines being very close to each other and this time we booked a hotel very close, which made the logistics much easier. It is often quite challenging to get to the start line in a foreign country, relying on public transport very early in the morning. Being close to the start line meant we could walk there (and buy coffee on the way).

Jerry was happy. He did not have to stand in the long portaloo line with me at the start and deal with an emotional wreck at the end. I highly recommend staying as close as possible to either the start or finish line if you travel away from home to an event. It is one less thing to worry about. We had hunted down great coffee the day before (thank you, "Intelligentsia") and I had eaten my pre-race banana and bagel.

The Bank of America Chicago Marathon is known for being a fast course with the race start and finish line in Grant Park near The Bean, a stunning work of public art in the heart of Chicago. The sculpture, officially called Cloud Gate, is one of the world's largest permanent outdoor art installations and made a great backdrop that day.

The tough year of 2013 was nearly behind me. I was so excited to be running that day; I had butterflies in my stomach, not the normal nerves. I had completed two marathon-training schedules in the same year and I was in peak condition. Regular massages and physiotherapy had paid off and I was injury free.

I ran my heart out in Chicago, pacing myself better than I had in London, remembering the negative split concept of running the first half of the marathon slower than the second. I went out slowly and finished fast. I was running more quickly than usual.

Choosing a marathon-training schedule involves determining your race day pace and, in the 12 or 16 weeks of training, you run with that pace goal in mind. On race day, many runners have their estimated pace times for every 5 km written down or printed on a wristband so they can easily see it as they run.

As I ran the streets of Chicago, I kept looking at my race pace on my running watch and checking it against my wristband, which was printed in a huge typeface, as I cannot read it without my glasses! I stuck to the plan. I had upgraded my watch since running in New York, so I knew the battery would not give up. Many ask me which running watch I use. There are so many varieties of great running watches out there and they change all the time so I suggest you read the reviews from other runners and treat yourself to a good one.

Chad again supported me with Julie (Jerry's wife) and they popped up everywhere on the course. It was an easy event for spectators to get around and it was great to see their smiling faces and the running banner. I remember very little of the Chicago scenery after The Bean, as I was so focused on my running and the pace and I was determined to achieve my goal this time.

I do remember very clearly, being a kilometre from the finish line when I saw Chad. I cannot speak highly enough or express enough gratitude to him for his wholehearted support of my running. He has been and continues to be at every race I run in. He carries the bags, stands for hours looking for me in a crowd of runners, wearing his silly hat and he never gets the line honours.

Chicago was no different, except that day I remember his broad smile, his cheers and encouragement as I only had 1000 metres left to run to finally achieve this massive goal. He knew how hard I had worked to get this far; he knew I was on track for a PB and he was willing me on, every step of the way.

I crossed the finish line of the 2013 Chicago Marathon in a time of 4:10:00 hours. My fastest time to date and nearly a Boston Marathon qualifying time. I had achieved all that I had set out to do and more that year.

There are so many reasons why I run. These change with every run, every event and who I am running with. Training for the Chicago Marathon had given me time to think and given me great clarity. It calmed me down and energised me, all at the same time. It made me a better listener and a better friend.

Running is much more than putting one foot in front of the other at speed!

Crossing the line of any marathon changes you and in achieving this one, I found and restored my faith in myself.

Life Lesson

Believe in yourself and then detach from the outcome.

CHAPTER SEVEN

2014 Boston Marathon #2

> The runners returned to Boston to reclaim the finish line.

In April 2014, I had the immense privilege and honour of running amongst the most courageous and strongest runners. It was never going to be our fastest marathon and it was never going to be the easiest, but it was always going to be the most memorable. From the moment we were offered the opportunity to return to Boston and run the 118th Boston Marathon in 2014, Helen and I were always going to do it, despite the many moments of hesitation.

The Boston Marathon is an iconic event for runners and not because of the bomb going off in 2013. This marathon started in 1897 and is the world's oldest annual marathon, held on the third Monday of April on Patriot's Day. One of the many reasons it is an iconic run is that in 1967, it was at the Boston Marathon that the first woman officially finished the full marathon, despite a man trying to pull her from the course. At that time, women were not allowed to run this distance. Undeterred and passionate, Katherine Switzer finished the race proving that women could run 42.195 km.

Three people had been killed, 264 wounded and many more had emotional scars after the horrific bombings on Boylston Street near the finish line in 2013. The runners and spectators and the City of Boston itself felt these scars.

One year on, Helen and I ran the 118th Boston Marathon and it had an even more profound significance, than the year before.

I was very nervous about repeating a marathon. I had said I would never do that. There seemed little point to me in repeating a run of that distance. I was wrong and learned that "never say never" is sometimes true! To date, I had not repeated a marathon but that changed with Boston #2.

Two of my major goals were now ticked off the list. I had completed running five marathons in five years and the Abbott World Marathon Majors series (or so I thought).

From the time that I had initially set this goal in 2010 to 2014, the Tokyo Marathon had been added to the Majors and so now there were six, not five, marathons to complete. The certificate for the five I had completed so far, was framed and on the wall at home, but Tokyo had now been added to my list. There was an enormous medal for completing all six and that little running voice in my head started talking to me again.

I was still a little uncomfortable saying that I had completed the course in 2013 and still felt a bit of a fraud. The 2013 Boston Marathon medal was now out of its packaging and displayed on my dresser, and I wanted it to count for something bigger so I made it part of a bigger goal.

I was going to complete ten marathons in ten years and complete the series by running Tokyo and I had no idea how. I had no idea which marathons I would run to make the ten in ten (apart from Tokyo) or the unbelievable ripple effect that this would create, but more on that in Chapter Ten when I completed the ten in ten. (Spoiler alert!)

With six marathons now completed, running the 2014 Boston Marathon could be number seven, but I was still a little hesitant. Then a few things happened, or as I like to think, some 'signs' cemented my decision and motivated me to return and run the Boston Marathon in 2014 and I am so happy that I did.

Helen's husband, David and Jerry said they would run it with us if we reran it. They contacted Travelling Fit, a great travel company for runners in Australia that guaranteed paid entries into many of these iconic races. As the popularity of marathon running has increased, many of the Major Marathons are now really difficult to get into, so companies like this will sell you a travel package that includes your race entry.

Coach Fi had been able to get us entries into the previous marathons, so we had never needed to use the company. We were fortunate and David and Jerry were both able to buy a Boston Marathon entry. The first sign!

The second sign came out running with Helen; she was still living in Melbourne and we rarely got to run together these days. We discussed crossing the blue and yellow line in Boston in 2014 and why we should return. We were both keen to complete what we had started the previous year but needed a more significant reason to repeat the run and the sixteen weeks of training.

I am sure it was one of Helen's ideas again and we decided that we should give back to the local Bostonian community, somehow. The locals had been through so much in the past year and had been so gracious to us on that horrible day. We wanted to give back to Boston, the community that had given us so much the year before. Giving back, in some way, seemed like a great reason to return to Boston and repeat the distance.

Marathon number one in Paris had been about breast cancer. Helen had lost her sister to this insidious cancer and we had found that having a more significant reason to run was a way of pulling through the challenging 35 – 40 km stage in the parks of Paris.

It was time to do the same again.

In those few hours catching up on each other's lives, watching another beautiful sunrise over Sydney, gulping down the gels and dealing with blisters and sore knees, I was reminded of why I run and why I had started.

Some days, running is about losing myself and allowing my head some space. On other days, it is about sharing the run with great friends; sometimes, it is just about getting the run done. Today was about sharing it with a great friend and remembering why we had started running in the first place.

Running has defined me over the years and now thinking about returning to Boston and how we could help make a difference in other people's lives, joined by David and Jerry, we found our reason to return.

Helen, a school principal, wanted to do something aligned with children and with the research done, we chose Dream Big! We had a plan! Founded in 2010, Dream Big! is a Boston-based non-profit organisation. Dream Big!'s mission is to help girls from low-income backgrounds achieve their dreams by providing them with the basic items and fees necessary to enable them to participate in sports and physical activities that contribute to their health, education and overall well-being.

Being part of Dream Big! also allowed us to be part of the local community, part of the Marathon Coalition, organised by an inspirational guy called Coach Rick. He had taken a group of charities and formed a much larger running community with a far-reaching impact.

Dream Big! was a perfect fit and our perfect motivation to embark on the gruelling training once more. When you are heading into the most challenging part of the training, running 30+ km on a Saturday morning and then sleeping for the rest of the day, it always helps to have a bigger reason to overcome the tiredness, the time commitment, the rigidity of life, work, training and just trying to fit everything into daily life.

The last few weeks of the training schedule, particularly for a marathon, are tough. The long runs dominate your life for weeks as you strategically plan work, social life and lots of sleep around them. Quality rest is just as important as running. We used to run Saturday mornings, so going out Friday night was not an option – I needed to be in bed early.

Up at the crack of dawn to beat the sun and heat, we would usually be finished 3-4 hours later. It was always tricky training in the southern hemisphere's summer and then flying to the United States for a marathon in April when it was often cooler.

Everyone tells you to train in the same gear as you will run in on race day, but to be honest, that is only sometimes possible when you go from summer to winter or from the southern to the northern hemisphere. I have always tried to plan around this with lots of layers, ensuring the undies, base leggings and running tops that I wear when I am training, are the same as I run in, on race day. Then I can just add layers like arm warmers and throwaway tops. This helps to prevent chafing.

Running around Sydney trying to fit in the long distances of over 30 km was also a challenge. Jerry's maps were fabulous, but even he had to make us do a few loops of Centennial Park just to ensure we got the total distance in and running in circles was always a challenge for me and would start the mind games.

Every good training plan needs reliable support. Chad would cycle all over the city to meet us all at various spots on the course with extra water and bananas. It was always great to take a few minutes rest when we found him on a corner with his bicycle parked and water in hand.

It would have been hard to do this training without such great support. I remember one of these long runs when we had miscalculated the distance and reached 32 km already that day but we still had a few kilometres left, to reach the usual coffee shop. We stopped our running watches and called Chad for a pickup. We were not running a metre more than we needed that day and when you complete some of your long runs, which I hope you do one day, you will know exactly how we felt!

The training was always followed by a late breakfast (or early lunch sometimes) discussing the race and why we had committed to it once again, inflicting this upon ourselves. We loved it when it was over! A long hot shower was promptly followed by a long nap. Saturdays were not much fun for the rest of the family.

I have said many times that the marathon training schedule prepares you to run the distance of a marathon, but it cannot prepare you for what happens on race day. I knew it would be emotional to return to this beautiful city, running the marathon a year on and overcoming the fear that it could happen again.

I could never have been prepared for the emotional impact that it had on me and continues to, to this day.

The training was completed without any major dramas and once again we packed our bags. A tip when travelling overseas for a marathon is always to pack your race gear in your hand luggage. Can you imagine if your running shoes and gear got delayed or lost in transit?

Long-haul flights present many other challenges, including jet lag, so we have always planned for a couple of nights' sleep on arrival to help adjust to the local time zone. I am also careful about what I eat on a plane and have been known to travel with my homemade ham sandwiches.

Being well-hydrated for a marathon the few days before the race is critical, so drinking enough water on the long flight is also an issue. We have solved this by buying a litre (or two) of water in the duty-free shop once you are past security and carrying electrolytes with us to pop into the water, for extra salts. The crew on the plane are usually great at re-filling them once they know why you need it!

There is an old saying, *"failing to plan is like planning to fail!"* We (try not to) leave anything to chance if we can plan it.

I was well prepared to run the 2014 Boston Marathon, but I was not prepared for the emotional events that preceded it. As we flew into Boston from Dallas, just a few days before, the gentleman I sat next to on the plane thanked me for returning to his city. Thanked me! Many Bostonians had wondered if the runners would return (as if we would not) and I began to feel overwhelmed by what we were setting out to do. We were going to reclaim the finish line of the Boston Marathon. I was crying before we even landed in Boston.

As we often did, the four of us checked out the finish line the day before the race and we saw the now-famous blue and yellow lines painted on the pavement. We would cross them in 24 hours. Another tear! Jerry then had the forethought to make us walk back 700 m from the finish line to the exact place we had stopped the previous year. So clever of him to help us face that emotion the day before rather than at 41.195 km, exhausted and hungry. More tears were shed.

The slogan *"Boston Strong"* was everywhere. It was created as part of the reaction to the Boston Marathon bombing. In the hours after the bombing on 15 April 2013, the slogan "*Boston Strong*" appeared as a highly popular hashtag on Twitter and rapidly spread worldwide to express Boston's unity after the bombing. The slogan showed up on T-shirts and other products. The Boston Bruins (an ice hockey team) displayed the slogan on their helmets at their game two days after the bombing and at the first baseball game in Fenway Park after the fateful day, the stadium announcer told the crowd:

"We are one. We are strong. We are Boston. We are Boston strong."

A car sticker with that slogan printed on it is still on the back of my car and reminds me every day that I, too, am strong.

Then another amazing thing happened. As we wandered around the city, I was overcome with emotion passing stores and street corners adorned with blue and yellow, the colours of the Boston marathon. We passed a church near the finish line and Helen and I were presented with a unique hand-knitted blue and yellow scarf. In addition to race jackets, hats and shirts purchased at the expo, many of the 2014 Boston Marathon runners received this heartfelt gift.

In February of that year, the Old South Knitters Club of the Old South Church on Boylston Street hatched the idea for the Marathon Scarf Project. The thought was to wrap runners in marathon blue and yellow scarves knitted with love and courage. The group's goal was to knit a few hundred, but the project went viral and by marathon weekend, they had more than 7,000 scarves handmade by knitters across the country and worldwide.

Some pieces were knitted, some were sewn and some had images on them. There were as many patterns as artists. But they were all handcrafted and came with a tag that included the name of the artist and where they were made.

During the marathon weekend, church volunteers laden with scarves stood in front of the Old South Church and one by one, runners were given the scarf of their choice and a blessing. This project had gone viral with knitters and it was the same with the runners that day.

It was unusually cold in Boston; the scarves provided runners with comfort, unity and remembrance. This priceless memento is on my dresser at home and reminds me daily of the moment the Boston community embraced us again.

Later that same day, I remember going to the pre-race pasta party. The Marathon Coalition hosted it and we met Coach Rick. Being careful what I ate (after Peita's experience), we also got to meet many local runners, all united by a common cause – to give back to Boston.

So much in my life that past year had changed, but somehow this was all so insignificant now. We travelled on the bus again to Hopkinton, but we shared the experience with David and Jerry this time. As we ran the city of Boston that day in the Dream Big! T-shirt, we had millions of supporters calling our names and shouting, "Dream Bigger, Gill and Helen!" It is so hard to describe the depth of my emotions that day.

The Wesley College supporters were there again, but I am sure they were louder and more excited this time than the year before.

We ran that day to give back to Boston, but we got so much more from that community than we gave. There was so much more at stake in Boston that day; the 42.195 km was the last thing on anyone's mind.

We ran that day with hearts full. David, Jerry, Helen and I crossed that blue and yellow finish line and the 2014 Boston Marathon medal was placed around our necks.

When I asked Helen about the 2014 Boston Marathon, her strongest recollection was a song.

"In 2014, Michelle Lewis released the song Run, Run, Run about her training for Boston. That song and music video became the soundtrack of my training and maybe my life for a while, but it never meant so much as when Michelle played it to welcome the amputee runners, Boston bombing survivors, to the stage at the pre-marathon celebration event. At that moment, I knew we were meant to return to Boston, where that marathon will always be so much more than a race," said Helen.

Jerry remembers running through a suburb of Boston, where they were sitting on the porch with guns.

"I remember the raw country feel at the starting line just outside Hopkinton, with people sat on their porches nursing shotguns and what a contrast it was to the cosmopolitan vibe of Boston just 42.195 km away – a bit of a metaphor for the marathon journey and how different you feel at the end, compared to the beginning."

David has never forgiven us for leaving him behind. We headed up a hill at around the 10 km mark and he dropped back a little. We could have waited. We should have waited, but we got caught up in the excitement.

But this marathon was never about ticking off my goal list or getting another medal. It was so that the runners could "claim back the finish line," and they did. The runners had returned not to win but to show humanity is stronger than terrorism.

'When the going gets tough, the tough go running.'

I have never been so inspired by humanity as I was that weekend. Bostonians welcomed the running community as family and their spirit returned.

Running every kilometre of the 118th Boston Marathon in 2014 I was surrounded by the strength and courage that sometimes gets thrown by the wayside as we sprint through life.

The things I talk about when it comes to marathon running, foot care, fighting that mental barrier, menopause, which shoes to wear and pre-race traditions, are all important to me. But when I sit down (which is not very often) and think about running – the one thing that I want to talk about, the one thing that I felt and saw in the 36,000 2014 Boston Marathon runners and the one thing I hope that I hope I have instilled in my children is, *"the importance of surrounding yourself with people who inspire you and people you can admire."* Runners, give me that!

Running is in my blood; it keeps me strong in so many ways. *#Boston Strong* will always be part of my life and I will continue to draw upon it when life gets tough and 2015 was about to get tough!

> **Life Lesson**
>
> If you fail to plan you plan to fail.

Chapter Eight

2015 Melbourne Marathon

> Running is much like life;
> It is not always sunshine
> and roses.

Running 16 km on Saturday was a real test of my mind versus my body.

Running 16 km used to be normal, never easy, but achievable; now it feels so hard.

Since being very ill earlier in the year, I find running challenging. Knowing it was achievable just months before makes it even harder.

One year on from the 2014 Boston Marathon and six months out from the 2015 Melbourne Marathon, my mind was seriously messing with my body and my running. I had been laid up in bed with a mysterious illness for several months. I had not run for weeks. There were some dark days when I wondered if I would ever run again.

I never really found out what was wrong with me other than I was "burnt out." I had spent weeks in bed, struggling to even get dressed, let alone run. My recovery had been slow and even short walks on the beach, felt like I was climbing a mountain. Shelby had been amazing; flying home to look after me and friends rallied with food drop-offs and cleaning my house.

I realised during this time that you do not have to struggle through these horrible events, on your own. It is ok to ask for help your friends want to help they just do not know how. The British blood in me was strong and I was not good at letting people know that I needed help.

The last few months had been tough and many around me had quickly blamed my burnout on running. I questioned myself as well. Had I done too much? Had I run too many marathons, overstretched myself with my heavy work schedule and everyday life stuff?

Chad had been ill, we had moved into our new home and I had run a half marathon in Auckland just days after the move. I was recovering from a flu bug at the time and running a half marathon, or any event for that matter, when you are sick, is not recommended.

Maybe, my friends were right – I had taken on too much. But running had always been a release from stress for me and I never felt that it added to it. Now I could not or did not want to run. My focus was on recovering from whatever it was (maybe a good old-fashioned nervous breakdown) and claiming back my health so that I could eventually run again and this goal helped me through some long, strange days.

Entering the 2015 Melbourne Marathon was a great focus and motivated me to get well and gave me a reason to get my health back on track. It gave me something to aim for rather than just dwelling on being sick. There were no huge costs for international flights like so many other races and no expensive accommodation to pay for.

The monetary investment of competing in an international marathon had previously motivated me, to ensure I never missed a training session, that I did not stay late at work and did not have that extra wine on a Friday night. I did not need the extra pressure this time! I had all the motivation I needed and that was to get healthy again. I did not have much annual leave and having used up all of my sick leave, I did not want to be away from work for too long, so a marathon on home soil made sense this year. Helen was still living in Melbourne, so this was a bonus.

Running in Melbourne also gave me an opt-out clause if I did not get fit enough in time. I do not usually like an excuse to bail; I like to push myself. This was a time when I did not need to push.

My newfound love of yoga was teaching me to be kind to myself; for once, I was listening. Many women focus on other people's needs before their own and forget to put the oxygen mask on themselves and I am no different, usually. This year was different. I was putting the oxygen mask on myself first.

I felt a bit better, enough to put on my shoes and head out the door. It was 25 April, ANZAC Day in Australia, as I nervously headed out for a run. ANZAC Day is when we remember those who have given their all, for their country, across Australia and New Zealand.

Running at the break of dawn was inspiring today, as I was thinking about all those who had given their lives, the ultimate sacrifice so that I could run freely across the Sydney Harbour Bridge that morning. The sun was just coming up across Sydney Harbour as I stopped on the Bridge to take a photo. The sunrise was breathtaking.

One of the many things I love about running is what I see before most others are out of bed. Today was no different.

Returning from the Dawn Service, men and women crossed the Sydney Harbour Bridge adorned in their medals, reminding me once again that we should appreciate every step we take. The streets are usually empty at this time of day, but today they were busy.

It was uplifting to have the freedom to run and to see so many proud, smiling faces, as they made their way home from the service. As a 9 km run turned into 10 km, my mind started to focus on the negative once again. The internal chatter started, "You cannot do this. This is too far. Best to turn back now." Just as I was about to give in to the noise in my head telling me to head for home, I ran past a giant poppy sculpture.

I love poppies; they grow in England in May, in springtime. May is my birth month, so I remember seeing them burst into flower around my birthday every year. The red poppy is a symbol of war remembrance the world over. People in many countries wear the poppy to remember those who have died in a war or are serving in the armed forces. In many countries, the poppy is worn on Armistice Day (11 November), but in Australia, it is most commonly worn on ANZAC Day.

Crowds lingered, as the artist who had created this sculpture explained his work and I took a few precious minutes to pause my watch and catch my breath, thinking about how grateful I was to be able to run again. After all, it is the journey, not the destination, or so they say.

I continued my run. Inspired, I managed to complete 16 km. It was the furthest I had run in many months. The battle between my mind and body had been constant for the past two hours, but I had overcome it thanks to the inspiring people I saw on the Bridge, the sculpture and because I had been listening to some great music on my iPhone.

I do not usually run with headphones as I love the peace and time to think things over, but sometimes, it gives me a much-needed distraction. I have a great running playlist.

Music has been very much a part of running for all of us. Helen referred to it in the last chapter. Jerry used to make a CD for each member of the running group. He would give it to us at our annual Christmas catch-up and the music always reflected the races we had done, the places we had visited and events from the year.

My playlist that day included all of these tracks and more. It is not your normal *Eye of the Tiger* tracks that many runners use but songs that have inspirational words and inspire me in some way. Today, thanks to Jason Mraz and his song *Living in the Moment*, I ran for longer than I had for months.

The run had been slow, but it did not matter. Today was about restoring my soul and my faith in myself. I changed the conversation in my head and my body won the battle today, as I had been focused on freedom, privilege, the journey and the magnificent sunrise over Sydney Harbour.

Over the coming weeks, my return to running continued to be a challenge, but that is the point of setting worthy goals. They are not supposed to be easy.

That Sunday afternoon, as I was recovering from the long run, I was inspired once again by Paula Radcliff, the elite UK runner.

Watching a very wet and cold 2015 London Marathon on television, I remembered when I had lined up to start the 2012 London Marathon just three years earlier. It had been cold that day, but there had been amazing crowds and a brilliant blue sky, much like it had been for all the marathons I had run to date. I did not take this for granted, the thought of rain for 42.195 km haunted me and I would find out why in 2019.

So why Paula Radcliffe? Why today, in April 2015?

At the time Paula held the World Record for the women's marathon distance over 42.195 km, a time of 2:25:25 hours that she had set some 13 years ago in London.

Today, she was lining up to run the 2015 London Marathon for her final competitive event at age 41. Inspirational in itself, she was recovering from major ankle surgery and Achilles tendon issues that we know of, but I am sure there would have been more injuries.

Paula had become a mother and she had been unable to run, for a much longer period than my short absence over the past few months. From only being able to run for five minutes, Paula had run her way back to an elite level and here she was running the 2015 London Marathon, completing it in 2:38:00 hours.

I have learned that sometimes you need to look outside yourself to get that extra kick of self-belief. It comes in the strangest of ways and when you are least expecting it. You just have to have an open mind and today, for me, it came from Paula Radcliff. As I watch her on the television, I am grateful, inspired and determined to continue the battle of my mind chatter versus my body and reclaim my health. I will run my way back, by completing the 42.195 km in Melbourne later that year. Melbourne Marathon, I am coming for you in some shape or form.

I have said previously that when you make it to the start line of a marathon, you are a champion in my eyes. What happens in the next few hours of the race, as you pound the streets, is a little beyond your control, as we found out in Boston in 2013 and we were about to find this out again.

Lining up at the start line means you have made it through anything from 12-20 weeks of training, worrying about every niggle your body throws at you, sacrificing more than a few social activities and maybe you have given up alcohol for a while. By now, friends are more than a little tired of you talking about the upcoming marathon. As you wait nervously at the start line before dawn, usually in the cold and dark, nothing else has been on your mind as much, as this moment in time.

Helen and I are at the start line of the 2015 Melbourne Marathon. The self-doubt that has plagued me all year has not gone and the little voice starts again, "Why are you doing this? Do you need to line up in that toilet queue again? Will you finish? What happens if you do not finish? "

I have to control the internal chatter more today than ever before and I have to find a way to change the conversation in my head. Positive self-talk and mixing with other runners helps, as does taking a few random photos and eating my chocolate raisins. Anything to distract myself.

Helen and I have completed our training remotely again and we know what will be will be. With luck and a few thousand steps, in four to five hours, we will cross the finish line of the 2015 Melbourne Marathon in the famous Australian stadium called the Melbourne Cricket Ground (MCG) and we will have another medal placed around our neck.

The Melbourne Running Festival is such a great event for runners. There are several other distances including a great 10 km, that are part of this running festival, as there are at most running events and the atmosphere is electric. We have run the half marathon distance a few times previously with KTP, our Sydney running group, but the Marathon is the premiere event.

This running festival holds some special memories, as it was the first running event that our Sydney running group had travelled to a few years ago. We had a great girls' weekend away with lots of laughs, great food, a little wine and a little running. It made me feel part of a community again, of something bigger. I had missed that since leaving the UK.

I talk mainly about the marathon distance in this book, but if that is not for you, please consider a shorter distance. Maybe a 10 km or a half marathon at one of these bigger running festivals to experience the atmosphere and camaraderie. You will not regret it. It is such fun.

We first entered this particular event to run through the famous athlete's tunnel into the MCG, hoping we would see ourselves on the big screen and run a lap of this iconic stadium. I remember being very excited the first time we did this at the end of a half marathon.

You enter a tunnel that is quite short, but one that you have seen on television many times if you live in Australia and follow sports. As you enter the stadium, you look up to the right and you can see yourself on the big-screen television. In the final few hundred metres of the race, the blisters and the exhaustion are forgotten, with the crowds in the stadium cheering you on as you run across the finish line. I was looking forward to seeing myself on this screen again today.

But I am getting ahead of myself. We must run the full marathon today before we experience the stadium and the medal.

I always knew today was going to be a slower marathon. I had realistic expectations, having had those few months sick in bed at the start of the year, but I knew I could complete it within the cut-off time. Most events have a cut-off time for the marathon, which is an excellent guide for slower runners. Event organisers publish the distance and the time you have to be at that distance by, as this is often when roads that have been closed for the event, reopen. At some events, they have a sweeper bus to pick up the stragglers and I was determined to be ahead of the bus and not in it.

The start was exciting, as always, as Helen and I try not to go out too fast – trying to keep a steady pace. We chatted, catching up on our news as we got through the first kilometre and settled into a gentle rhythm. We got into the groove as we always do. We ran around Albert Park and headed down Fitzroy Street, towards St Kilda and the sea, out to Port Melbourne and back towards the city. We were heading towards Melbourne and the finish line when our marathon took a turn for the worse.

I had always known that I would struggle with this marathon and I was ok with that. Helen had been happy to run at my slower pace. We had run down St Kilda Road and turned into the Domain. We were at around the 35 km mark, which I always find very tough, as this is when the mind has to do most of the work. The body has had enough. Helen unexpectedly turned to me and said, "I am not feeling so good."

At that moment, the adrenalin shot through my body. I was not tired anymore. Helen had never said that before in a race. This was serious. Coming back from my breakdown, I had always thought I might have an issue today, but it was not me. It was Helen! My heart was in my mouth. I did not know what to do. I was terrified. This felt worse than the Boston experience because this was my best friend and she was not doing so well.

Once in training, we had stopped running as her heartbeat went through the roof, but her husband David had been there. This time it was just me, so I tried to remain calm and asked quietly if this was the same issue. It was.

There was no way I would be able to deal with this on my own. At 34 km I was seriously fatigued, but somehow our amazing bodies can find that extra inner strength when we really need it. I could see the first aiders in the distance and asked Helen again, as calmly as I could, "Can you make it a few more metres to the first aiders just up there?" I did not wait for an answer. We kept running.

The first aiders were quick to help as Helen explained the issue to them. She was in complete control. Helen was truly amazing.

We had been running for over four hours and were exhausted, but she took complete control of the situation. She knew her body and how to treat herself and told the first aiders, in no uncertain terms, what she was going to do. "I am going to lay down by this tree with my legs in the air and wait for my heart rate to slow down and to click back in."

I would never recommend second-guessing a first aider, but Helen knew her body and knew what she needed to do. A few minutes passed and nothing changed. Running watches on pause (once again), I began to wonder if our race that day was run.

As the first aiders rightly began to consider taking her to the hospital, I called David, her husband, who was waiting in the stadium for us to finish. I needed his help. David had already run the half marathon that day and just finished the 21.195 km, but he was so quick to act. David ran 7 km back to find us. I asked the first aiders to wait for him to arrive, as I was in no fit state to make these decisions for Helen. I have never been so happy to see David running towards me as I was that day and at last, I took a few deep breaths.

As David arrived to find Helen still with her legs up a tree, she jumped up and said, "It's ok, it's back in. Now we can finish the race!" Her heart, which had been out of rhythm, was now back in rhythm. Her heart rate was normal again. Nothing was going to stop her now.

Helen was determined to finish this marathon. On her feet, the waiver signed and leaving the first aiders speechless, Helen started her watch, I started mine and we started to run again. Grateful to have David by our side (just in case), the three of us ran the final 7 km in silence, each digging deep, trying to process what had just happened. As we ran through the athlete's tunnel, we saw ourselves on the big screen television, we heard the crowds cheering and we finally crossed the finish line together, with a time of 5:15:06 hours.

Another marathon, another lesson learned. So much of what we think is within our control is not, whether it is life or running marathons. But *'when the going gets tough, the tough go running.'* All the training in the world would not have prepared either of us for that moment, but we rose to the challenge. We were both so tired, but we know each other so well; we had run many kilometres together over the years and we knew we could trust each other. We respected the decisions each of us made and knew we had each other's backs.

The post-marathon celebration that night was a little low-key as we processed the events of that day, the year and all that we had both been through. We were so grateful to have finished the race. It did not break us. It would make us stronger. Helen was subsequently diagnosed with Atrial Fibrillation and, after surgery, went on to run her next marathon in 2017 when we returned to New York.

The self-doubt that had plagued me all year had gone and the extra kick of self-belief I got that day certainly came in the strangest of ways. Once again, the marathon distance tested me and showed me that I am much stronger than I think I am and that running truly is much like life; *it is not always sunshine and roses.*

The number eight marathon was now complete. I only had two marathons left to run and four years to complete them. The goal was in sight.

> **Life Lesson**
>
> Practice gratitude, it will never let you down.

CHAPTER NINE

2017 San Francisco Marathon

> Running a marathon is not easy, but it is immensely rewarding and character-building. Running helps me to control the constant chatter going on in my head.

I love the structure and discipline that training for a marathon gives me. It is January 2017 and I am so excited. I have signed up for the 2017 San Francisco Marathon to be held in July. I am on track to complete ten marathons in ten years, with only two more to run and two years to do it.

Helen and I had planned to run this marathon together, but as we all know, life sometimes gets in the way of the best-laid plans. My ninth marathon entry was in. San Francisco is not part of the World Marathon Majors, so it is pretty easy to enter by applying online and I got an instant place. You might question why I was excited about the opportunity to run all those hills for fun, but it was a step closer to a bigger goal.

My hotel booking is made and the international flights are booked. Then, Helen returned from a summer walking holiday, having sprained her ankle. Realising her recovery was slow; she went for a scan and discovered that she had broken a bone in her foot. Helen had to focus on the long game of being able to run well into her eighties, as this was far more important to her than running the San Francisco Marathon in just five months.

I was faced with a choice. I could cancel or postpone my entry as I still had plenty of time to complete the goal. I had not run a marathon in 2016 and the chatter in my head told me that if I left it much longer, I might lose my nerve or even the ability to do it.

I was slowly learning to listen to the little running voice in my head and it was loud about San Francisco. I was committed to the bigger goal. I would run the 2017 San Francisco Marathon and complete marathon number nine. I am eternally grateful that I listened to the chatter, made the choice to run and did not wait for the red light to turn green, and you will find out why in the next chapter. I was excited, keen and committed and I would not let the self-doubt surface again.

Returning to the mindset of training for a marathon is hard, but it only takes a few weeks for my body to realise that we are going to run 42.195 km again. I was trying to work out if I should train for twelve, sixteen or twenty weeks. All time frames work – twelve weeks of training had worked for me in the past and I knew that I was now fit enough to train for a marathon in that time. This would mean less chance of getting injured, which had worked for me in previous marathons.

Then the internal chatter started; "twelve weeks was not long enough, I would not be ready, it was not enough training to get to the finish line. It may have worked before, but sixteen weeks was better for a more solid foundation." It is funny to think that I still question myself and my ability, even though I have done this eight times!

As I was having these internal conversations, I realised I was just procrastinating, putting off the inevitable. It was time! I looked at the calendar and it was sixteen weeks from the race. I sat down, entered all the training sessions into my calendar and started training. The sixteen-week schedule would allow a few extra weeks to build up to the longer distances more gradually if I needed it. I began to dream about crossing another finish line. I would be mentally and physically better prepared.

Many experts say to start training for a marathon, you should be able to run 10 km as a good base. As I have been running for a few years now, I was consistently running that distance once or twice a week, so I spent March slowly building up the distances from 10 km to 12 km, 14 km and 16 km. I focused on steady runs every Saturday, getting used to going to bed early on Friday night and beginning once again to watch what I ate, cutting out the junk food that does not fuel my running. I did some shoe research and purchased some new trainers (shoes) for the event (any excuse).

The new trainers will last me sixteen weeks of training, all 800 km + and the 42.195 km of the race. It is essential to have new shoes to ensure they last that distance, or so I tell myself. I donate my old shoes to a local running store that collects them for an overseas charity and I am ready.

I also purchased my first ever camelback, a hydration backpack for runners. The camelback allows me to carry enough water and food that I will need in the race and on the long runs as I am now training for this marathon on my own and it seems a little unfair to expect Chad to support every training run. I am also discovering that I do not like water fountains or bubblers, as we call them in Australia. I cannot always rely on them to be working and I wonder how clean they are. The camelback will mean I can add my preferred electrolytes and can drink water when I want in the race and I do not have to wait until I reach an aid station.

The San Francisco Marathon is held in July each year in the northern summer, which means I am training through the latter part of summer in Sydney and I drink a lot of water when I run.

Many people have asked me what I eat during training, the race and recovery. We often eat a big bowl of spaghetti carbonara the night before a long training run. It is a good carbohydrate meal and quick to make so that I can get to bed early and the family loves it. The rest varies a little.

On the morning of a long run, I generally get up at least 30 mins before I run to have a coffee, eat a banana and go to the toilet - in that order! On race day, I add some protein with cream cheese on a plain bagel for extra energy and sometimes a Cliff Bar (a healthy muesli bar).

Carrying my water has meant that I can add electrolytes to my water, which helps prevent me from cramping. All running shops have a great selection of these and I have tried most of them. They can upset your stomach, so it is a great idea to train with them so that you do not have any nasty surprises like unplanned bathroom stops on race day. I use products called Tailwind or Nuun tablets at the moment. The other good tip is to check who the race sponsor is and what electrolytes will be at the aid station on race day. Try these on a few of your training runs as well.

During a long run, I have tried many running gels for the extra fuel you need when you are out there for hours. You will need them on race day to stop you from hitting that imaginary wall that everyone talks about. I have never hit the wall as start to eat at five kilometres and keep eating every five kilometres—no weight loss for me. Gels, Cliff Blocks, jelly babies, chocolate raisins and snakes (the sweets, not the reptiles) are what I rely on. I carry a variety of these with me, as the distraction of eating and the different tastes help me with the mind chatter at the latter end of the race.

I even have a friend who runs with peanut butter and jam sandwiches. It is a case of training to eat what works for you and your stomach. After a long run, one thing that has not varied much is my poached eggs on toast and a hot black coffee for breakfast. Good protein, carbohydrates and great caffeine hit work wonders before the long afternoon nap.

You should not have to be a nutritionist to be healthy. It is not meant to be complicated and confusing. Yet it often is. I say, go back to basics!

Over the various marathons, I chatted with Brenda, very much part of my support crew now, following the great help that she gave me after my breakdown before the Melbourne marathon. Brenda's approach comes from the wise woman's tradition of healing – eat what your great-grandmother ate! For a high-performance diet, she recommends that you choose homegrown veggies and eggs when possible; homemade meals for maximum nutrition and minimal bad stuff; nourishing and aromatic dishes that get your juices going; warm foods in winter, cold in summer; nutritious good fats like grass-fed butter, heavenly duck fat, fragrant olive oil and smooth coconut oil; saving small treats for special occasions including coffee! (I may have ignored that one!)

To build or rebuild your body, especially while you are training, she had me eating beautifully prepared meats, delicious sour foods like yoghurt and sourdough, wild-caught seafood and fish and plenty of amazing eggs (I raise chickens now as a result). To cleanse and alkalise my body, I was *trying* to eat fermented and fresh vegetables, fresh and cooked whole fruit and drink plenty of water. Not too many rules. Maximum joy. Simple!

I am also a consistent taker of high-quality nutritional supplements.

The final few weeks of training are known as tapering. I mentioned this in an earlier chapter, but maybe a little more information is needed. Tapering is when you ease off the training (a little). Cutting back on the mileage allows your tired body to rest and get some much-needed energy back in the legs.

All good training programmes have this built into the schedule. So, if you stick to the plan and do not run any more than the plan tells you, you will be well-rested by race day. You need to sleep more and eat well during tapering. During those last three weeks of training, your body needs to rest, recover and prepare for the big day.

It can mess with the little voice in your head when you only go out for a shorter run, but I know tapering is critical for me, so I do not listen to the voice. I sleep a lot, shop more (I never know what to do with the extra time I have on my hands when I am not running) and eat well. I am small-framed, so just "carb loading" (or stuffing yourself full of carbohydrates) the night before does not work for me. I "carb load" the whole week before a race and love the extra pasta and pizza, knowing I will need the extra fuel on race day.

Running a marathon is not easy, but it is immensely rewarding and character building and I have learnt to control the constant questioning that goes on in my head.

"I've done this before! That doesn't mean you can do it again!"

"Should I run on a treadmill today as it's raining?"

"Will running on a treadmill cause more or fewer injuries? It may aggravate the Achilles issue; it has done before."

No matter how many events you have run (in my experience), the should and should not, the "yin and yang" voices in your head, are always present and you just have to train yourself to control them. It is a little like imposter syndrome for runners and learning how to manage mental chatter is as important, as the physical training.

Race day is the day when the weeks of daily discipline pay off. The mental toughness of daily training, good sleep patterns, a few missed nights out and the relentless focus on good nutrition all contribute to the moment you line up at dawn and wait for the starting gun to go off.

Every marathon I have run has inspired me and strengthened me in some way and I knew San Francisco would be no different.

Race day is just that; it is just one day. What will be will be! From running over the past ten years, I have learned that as long as you are prepared for the unexpected, you will get to the end (of pretty much anything). That is why it is character-building.

The Boston bomb, Helen's cardiac issue at 35 km in Melbourne, the bathroom incidents that I have never discussed here (trust me, you do not want the details), the weather, the injury niggles on race day that appear from nowhere and the cobblestones on the course that you had no idea existed, are all real.

In the end, it makes little difference if I have trained for twelve, sixteen or twenty weeks; it is still hard. The shoes you wear and the injuries are less important than you realise; the events on the day teach me time and time again that *"if it is to be, it is up to me"* and my mind works out how to deal with it.

This can be exciting when you learn to let go of the outcome, knowing most of what will happen is beyond your control and you can rise to the challenge.

The starting line for San Francisco was different to all of the others so far. I was the only one running from my running group this time, so Chad came with me to the start to keep me company. He even managed to line up with me in the starting corral for a while (with no intention of running), which was quite funny as we stood there in the fog and watched the sunrise laughing together. It did help to calm my nerves.

I had not thought about how cold it might be in July as it was summer. I was expecting heat and planned for a warm run. I went shopping the day before, to buy an extra layer of clothing that I planned to discard along the way, but I ran with this new hoodie for the whole race. I usually discard my jumper at the start of the marathon, where they are collected and given to charity. Since Boston in 2013, the anxiety of being cold at 41 km has never left me. I always carry a sweater and tie it around my waist as I run, just in case I need it.

The fog made it very cold as I ran across the Golden Gate Bridge. I could not see a hand's length in front of me. I took a selfie to send to Helen and to try and distract myself. It was cold and foggy and I had the yellow Uniqlo hoodie pulled tight over my head. I looked ridiculous, but I did not care.

Across the bridge, we ran through a beautiful park and I ducked into an actual toilet rather than using a portaloo. When I came out, the sun was shining. The fog had lifted and the sun had just popped out. The run back across that bridge was amazing. I could see it this time. I was on fire. I had trained well for those San Franciscan hills.

Or so I thought. At about the half-marathon mark, I had a "blinding flash of the obvious." Here was the lesson this marathon was going to teach me. I had trained for hours running *up hills*, but I had not trained to run down them. You may think that running downhill is much easier and it is. But when you do a lot of downhills (like I was today), you use different muscles and these muscles needed training; otherwise, they hurt. A lot!

I did not know whether to laugh or cry. How could I not have planned for this? The second half of the marathon was not so much fun. I was OK on the flat. I was fine on the up-hills. I was in agony on the downhills. Unexpected niggles plagued me from 21.195 km with knee pain and my ITB (iliotibial band), which had not caused any training problems, started to hurt. But the weird foot pain that had been with me for most of the training miraculously disappeared. Go figure!

I had started the training for San Francisco with the thought that running this marathon was just about getting number nine done so that I could move on to number ten.

I was so wrong. It had so much more to teach me!

As I eventually crossed the finish line of the 2017 San Francisco Marathon in a few seconds under five hours, the pain dissipated. I was ecstatic. I had immersed myself in solo training, discovering new podcasts and subscribing to an Audible account. I had listened to so many great books. This marathon increased my confidence and courage and my mindset muscle was much more robust.

I was ready to complete marathon number ten in 2018 until events took an unexpected turn and got even more exciting.

> **Life Lesson**
>
> Develop strong mind muscles as well as strong physical muscles.

Chapter Ten

2017 New York Marathon #2

> Running a marathon with both of my children was beyond my wildest dreams and the biggest ripple effect of running.

"Mum, do you want to run the 2017 New York Marathon with me later this year?" asked Shelby on a late-night phone call from South Africa. Shelby was working for World Vision then and had been offered two World Vision charity places to run the marathon later that year. I was thrilled that she wanted me to do it with her.

It would involve fundraising, a lot of fundraising; we would need to raise $14,000. Shelby had seen first-hand the difference those funds could make when travelling in Kenya. She had met Jane, a 25-year-old woman whose life had been transformed thanks to a modern, lightweight wheelchair given to her by World Vision.

I said, *"Yes,"* without a moment's hesitation or self-doubt. The opportunity to run a marathon with my daughter, run around the streets of New York once again and cross the finish line of my tenth marathon in ten years with her was truly amazing.

And at the same time, we could make a difference in someone's life!

I knew not to wait until all of the lights were on green. I had just completed the 2017 San Francisco Marathon and was now signed up for another marathon in the same year. Poor Chad was rolling his eyes once more. I had twelve weeks to train.

Plenty of time.

As if that was not exciting enough, I called Ben, my son, now living in London and told him what Shelby and I would do. A few days later, he called to say, *"I'm in! I will run with you both as well."* Sibling rivalry is real in my family.

I would complete my goal of running ten marathons in ten years by crossing the finish line of the 2017 New York Marathon with both of my children.

I had never imagined running a marathon with one of my children when I started running back in 2007, but running a marathon with both of my children was beyond my wildest dreams and the biggest ripple effect of running by far. It was going to be very exciting and emotional when we crossed that finish line together.

Now fully recovered and not wanting to be left out, Helen called Travelling Fit. She would run with us and be there as well when I completed my goal. Shelby, now living in Melbourne, could train with Helen and the ripples of running spread.

Our training commenced and so did the text messages from London.

Week One of training and Ben's first SMS read: *"I have done my long run of 4.5 km and I am feeling great!"*

Little does he know that he will be doing this distance with his eyes closed in just over a week. He will not run anything less than that for the next 12 weeks. Being young and with no fear or self-doubt, he has decided 12 weeks of training is enough.

Waking up the following morning (there is a nine-hour time difference between Sydney and London), the next SMS reads, *"Will I be able to fly or even walk the day after the marathon? I am thinking about flying to Miami."* I am not sure what was going through his head, but it made me laugh.

They keep coming: *"Can I run with a cold?"*

"I've looked at the registration. It is very expensive! Shall I run for charity instead?"

"What?" I messaged back, *"You're not even registered yet!"*

A few weeks later, his flights are now booked, and he entered the race and messaged to say he had run 10 km. *"It was very slow Mum and I walked three or four times!"*

The 42.195 km is going to be a long way for Ben.

A few days later, he calls, *"I went out for my 22 km long run today, but I only did 12 km. I ran out of energy and my legs wouldn't go. I don't think I ate enough."* I was laughing and at a loss for words.

The road to New York was not going to be easy for him, or me as it turned out, but for other reasons. One of the many things I have learned along this marathon journey, is even though the schedule for training may look the same, the process is always different. This one was going to be very different for me.

Shelby was running with Helen in Melbourne and trying to manage shin splints, a common running injury, as best she could. Ben was (sort of) training solo in London.

I was training solo in Sydney. I had torn a calf muscle. It was the first major injury I thought might stop me from completing the goal this time. I encountered many obstacles as I worked towards the ten-in-ten goal, but this one tested me big time.

So, what do you do when Mark, the physiotherapist, says, *"Do not run!"* You cycle – indoors and out and you walk – a lot! Mark, who has been running competitively for 32 years and has an impressive 2:33:00 hour marathon finishing time, adjusted one of his online training plans for me.

Chad set up my bike on the indoor trainer in the spare room. The indoor trainer is a stand designed for an outdoor bike that turns it into a stationary one so that you can cycle indoors and go nowhere.

I put a towel on the floor under the bike because, for some reason, I sweat more on a bike than I do on a run and I did not want to ruin the carpet. I set the television up in front of the bike. There are no trees in my spare room, no birds to listen to, no traffic to distract me, just space. I needed something to break the monotony of cycling. I downloaded a spin class on YouTube.

For me, there was so much more fuss setting up the indoor bike and I do not like wearing padded cycling shorts. They make me feel like I am wearing a nappy (or diaper), but they do stop me from getting such a sore bottom when I sit on the bike saddle.

I am organised, gears ready, Netflix is good to go and I pedal.

I do not love cycling like I love running. I sweat for sure and I know it keeps my fitness up without increasing my injury and my heart rate is up. I was just not passionate about it.

I listen to the instructor, watch the television and keep looking at my heart rate and watch – five minutes left, four minutes, three minutes!

I rarely find myself willing or wishing for a run to end. Generally, I would keep going if I did not have to go to work or it was not getting too dark.

But cycling? I was wishing the 45 minutes away. I hope this will change; otherwise, training for the New York Marathon will be tougher than I thought. Goal setting comes with obstacles and I had to find a way to stay on track so that I could run around New York City.

Chad and I went cycling outside for a couple of hours on the weekend to change it up and it was much more fun than cycling indoors. Being outside made the time pass faster than the 45 minutes indoors! But again, it is so much more complicated.

Putting the bike rack on the car, transporting the bicycles to a safe place to ride and then parking and unloading the bikes at the other end. Do not get me wrong, I love cycling a path or trail, but in the city where I live, it is just impossible and I am scared of all the traffic chaos. The helmet, the gloves and the knicks (cycling shorts) are not flattering and I have never learned to ride a bike with clip-on cycle shoes. I cannot go cycling outdoors during the week when I come in late from work, so I keep going with the stationary bike in the spare room.

Cycling is one way to keep me on track with my training for the 2017 New York Marathon and I am sticking with it. I am learning to find new ways to train for this event because I am so dedicated to achieving it. This new motivation is helping me to overcome these obstacles and look at them differently. Nothing will stop me from crossing the finish line with my children. I power walk the long runs. It takes me all day.

With six weeks to go, I am boarding a plane for a work trip in Europe. I had originally planned some great long runs in Paris and London and a half marathon in my hometown of Bournemouth, with Ben and Steph, my niece. The torn calf muscle is slowly healing, but it is still sore; even walking the lengths of the airport this morning made me grimace.

Every marathon has thrown up a new challenge and New York #2 is no different, except that the challenge has come before race day. Doubt creeps in. "Will it be healed in time? Will I even make it to the start line?" Mark, my physiotherapist (also a runner), is confident it will be and I should trust him by now; after all, he has helped me through the last nine marathons. Me? I am not as confident.

"Will I be able to run the 42.195 km around New York streets without running at all for ten weeks, without doing any of the traditional training? Will I cross the finish line with the kids as planned?"

Complacent – how complacent I have been for the last nine years. But with that deep sense of knowing, "I will be ok! I will cross the line, somehow!" I continue cycling and walking.

In my heart, I know I can do this. I will give it my best shot. I will keep up the cycling, walking and climbing numerous stairs, but I will not run (yet). I have to respect this injury and what it is trying to teach me:

- *Not to be fearful*
- *You can do it*
- *It is just different*
- *You are resilient*
- *It is just another challenge you will overcome*
- *It is a true test of your passion for running.*

As I checked in for my flight today, the flight attendant enquired what I would do for the six-hour layover in Hong Kong.

I told her I had arranged to go to a hotel gym at the airport to train. "I am running the New York Marathon in a few weeks," I said confidently, leading to a few minutes of engaging conversation.

"I wish I could run," she said.

"Anyone can run," I replied.

"But I have issues," she returned.

"We all have issues," I said, my calf muscle reminding me of mine.

This conversation is a common one. Many people tell me they cannot run because of bad knees, because of big boobs, because they run out of puff. They are all real issues, but most can be solved if your desire to overcome them is big enough.

Sitting on the plane, I looked for a good movie to occupy me during the eight-hour flight to Hong Kong. I came across a documentary called *Free to Run*.

Here it is, another sign. The signs keep coming at me in different ways, reassuring me. It is weird how every time I register for my next marathon, I see a runner with a shirt on from that same event the previous year. Today someone on my flight was wearing a 2016 New York Marathon shirt. How does that happen?

The movie was another sign. The documentary reminds me that it was just 50 years ago, that women were not allowed to run marathons. That is in my lifetime. I am 57. These women did not take it for granted as I do. Many women before me, have paved the way to enable me to do what I love. They ran the streets so that I could have the opportunity to do this race.

Avon (a famous direct selling company) paved the way for female runners like me, by holding women's only running races across the USA and the UK before women could eventually compete for the marathon Olympic Gold medal in 1984; I got married in 1984. Men had been able to compete since 1896. I had no idea that this iconic company, which empowers women to take care of their financial security by building an entrepreneurial business from home, also helped put women's running on the map.

The documentary also showed Kathrine Switzer fighting her way into the Boston Marathon in 1967 and returning to Boston on her 70th birthday to rerun the distance. That will be me. I will run more marathons past my tenth (but maybe I will not tell the children that just yet as they think this will be my last one). I renew my commitment to:

Complete the ten marathons in ten years

Run the six Abbott World Marathon Majors and I added a new one,

To keep running when I am 60+ and 70+!

In the meantime, I have to learn to respect my body, do more yoga and take up swimming and cycling. I want to be free to run and run when I want to run for as long as I want to run.

Free to Run. Running Free. Training for New York #2 is trying (trying) to teach me patience!

Carrying running gear in my hand luggage so that I can cycle in the airport hotel gym is a small sacrifice. I head towards that stationary bike with renewed enthusiasm.

Heading into New York, my training had been very limited. The half marathon in Bournemouth that I was going to run with Ben and Steph turned into a long walk. I was determined to be part of this event, held in my old hometown, but I could not run.

Ben and I walked it for three hours. We were just in front of the sweeper bus that collects slow runners who will not complete the course in the cut-off time. (Not in it, thankfully!) We had a great day. We chatted all the way, still beat some runners and got another medal.

The 2017 New York Marathon ranks as one of the best days of my life. My lack of running made no difference to our amazing few days. Sharing this experience with my adult children and Helen, once again, was a day I will never forget and one that I find very hard to express in words. Who knew when I showed up at that oval one cold winter's night in July 2007 that I would be in New York running my tenth marathon with both of my children in 2017?

We again headed to the running expo to buy marathon merchandise and collect our race bibs. This was all new to Shelby and Ben, making it very exciting for Helen and me. We took so many photos.

Shelby was pretty organised and had brought warm clothes with her, for the starting line the next day. Ben was not organised. He had no warm clothes and as I mentioned in the earlier chapter about New York, you have to get across to Staten Island very early in the morning as they close the Verrazzano-Narrows Bridge for the runners to cross. You stand around for hours, waiting for the race to start. It is November and it is very cold.

Ben wandered around the stalls at the expo and bought himself what can only be described as a white paper "hazmat" suit. This would keep him warm and he could discard it at the start line. It was hilarious and kept all of us amused for hours.

Getting to the start line for the New York Marathon is quite tricky. We caught a train to the ferry terminal, a ferry across to Staten Island and then a long walk to the starting corrals. All of this, with Ben in his white paper suit.

As we waited a few hours until the start of the marathon, Shelby was in her charity shop ski suit to keep her warm and was doing some strange exercises called crab walking. This was to activate her glute muscles and prevent her shin splints from giving her too much grief during the race but it was very funny to watch. Ben stood around in his hazmat suit. The start line was a lot more fun for Helen and me this time.

We all crossed the start line together, but with the huge crowds, it was impossible to run the whole race as a group of four. We quickly split up. For the next five hours, I ran with Ben. Shelby and Helen went on in front; I knew I had to go easy and did not want to hold them up. Ben had said he would stay with me.

To this day, I am not sure if he was being gracious or had not done enough training! Mark (my physiotherapist) had given me a race day plan that meant walking for half a mile and then running for half a mile. This would prevent my calf tear from flaring up and give me the best chance of reaching the finish line. Slow and steady was my race plan. It is New York, so the distance is measured in miles. They have water stations every mile, which made sticking to the walking and running split easy and the race plan worked. I was well prepared mentally.

The 2017 New York Marathon was never about time; it was all about enjoying the journey and the experience.

It was a truly amazing day. Over three million spectators cheered us on. Chad and other friends were on the sidewalk, cheering and taking photos. Sharing the experience and the 26.2 miles with your children and best friend was and still is to this day, magnificent. This moment was worth every moment of the years of training and sacrifice that I had to make to get here.

Ben ran slowly (now without the ridiculous suit) and I ran a little and then walked fast. We chatted the whole race. We crossed the finish line in Central Park in just a little over five hours, a few minutes behind Shelby and Helen.

We had crossed the finish line of the 2017 New York Marathon. We had done it! Four very different runners, from three different cities; four very different training schedules and all with very different running backgrounds. We had worked together as a remote team to achieve this goal, which was so personal and different to each of us.

The post-race celebrations went long into the night with lots of Billy Cart French Champagne and French fries consumed by all. My husband, who is not one for gift giving, gave me a Tiffany charm bracelet with a New York Marathon charm on it to commemorate the achievement of my goal; ten marathons in ten years and for overcoming the many obstacles I had endured over the years. I could not have been happier.

Ben did fly to Miami the next day and he could walk.

The exhilaration of completing the goal was, however, surpassed that day by the fact that we had raised over $16,000 for World Vision. What a worthy cause!

That, in turn, was surpassed by running the distance with Shelby and Ben. I knew what it had taken for them to do this with me. The memories of that day still give me goosebumps.

I had never dreamed of this ripple effect of running, let alone imagined it possible.

Years later, as I write this book, I asked Shelby and Ben to share their thoughts on running the 2017 New York Marathon that may help you find your reason to give running a go. It does not matter what distance. They both went into the training for different reasons; they had unique experiences and learned different lessons. It will be the same for you when you try it.

Shelby – Why Did You Run the Marathon?

> *I ran for Jane and all children with disabilities who do not get an equal chance just because of where they were born.*
>
> *I ran to be with Mum when she ran her tenth marathon and to be a part of her big dream.*
>
> *I ran to make lifelong memories.*
>
> *I ran because the opportunity was too perfect not to. Being offered the last two spots on the World Vision team by a friend at a disability inclusion meeting in Georgia seemed too random, too perfect to tell the Universe, no.*
>
> *I ran to prove to myself that I could.*

> I ran for the training and the reason was to pull me away from my desk.

Ben – Why Did You Run the Marathon?

> Firstly, I ran to achieve a major goal while my Mum achieved her major goal.

> Secondly, I wanted to do a marathon because I saw it as pretty much the ultimate achievement in fitness. At the time, I wanted to get fit.

> Finally, I had been very busy at work and had forgotten to get Mum a birthday present before going overseas, so committing to run a marathon with her was a great last-minute gift!

Shelby – What did you enjoy?

> I enjoyed fundraising and creating a community around it while raising awareness of the great and essential work I am passionate about. It makes a huge difference for a small cost.

> Training with Helen in the long, dark, Melbourne winter. Sunset runs around Albert Park and sunrise runs along the Yarra River.

> The race! The cheering! The incredible atmosphere!

> The solidarity with the people of New York!

> The support crews. Dad, David and my friend Dionne were all on the side streets cheering us on.

> Ben's white paper outfit!

Ben – What did you enjoy?

> *I enjoyed seeing London. Living in London at the time, I did not consider how much of the city I would see, but as you get to the pointy end of the training programme and you are running a 30 km-long run, you see a considerable amount of the city. Running around Hyde Park, Big Ben, Buckingham Palace etc., was a great way to explore.*
>
> *I enjoyed the discipline of running three times a week.*
>
> *Seeing New York. Running my first (and only marathon) in New York was a great way to see that city as well. And it was a great excuse for a holiday in America.*
>
> *The relaxing feeling afterwards. There is nothing better than knowing you have done the work, achieved the goal and then you can relax, eat steak and drink beer.*
>
> *Knowing you are in the best shape of your life and have earned a good break and some indulgence.*
>
> *Five years on and the feeling has not faded; I am still enjoying a good, long break from running and I am still indulging.*

Shelby – What did you dislike?

> *The injuries. I had so many needles in my butt to manage the injury.*
>
> *The hours of painful shins, huge blisters and endless experiments with shoes, socks, podiatrist and warm-up exercises.*

Ben – What did you dislike?

There was nothing I hated.

Training at the start was hard. The hardest part of training is when you are not fit. It is far harder to go from being able to run 500 m to 5 km than it is to go from 5 km to 25 km.

Long runs can get boring. Training alone inevitably means running three to four hours on your own and whilst some great podcasts kept me entertained (shout out to the Dollop), I still got bored with the monotony.

Shelby – What did you learn?

Nothing can prepare you for these types of experiences. I have no words for how much fun five hours of running in the rain was! I would re-do every moment again tomorrow if I could.

It had been years of inspiration, months of training, late nights of fundraising and hours of physiotherapy, but the four of us made it to the finish line.

Everything is possible when you put your mind to it.

Ben – What did you learn?

Honestly, not a huge amount.

Before I started training, the idea of a marathon seemed like a close-to-superhuman feat, but I guess I learned that it is something I can do.

And do, with only a couple of months of training (sorry, mum, I was very slow to get started).

For me, a marathon was a huge goal, but it is now an achieved goal.

The final words come from Shelby:

"Life is just a collection of moments... and this is one of the most incredible I have ever experienced. Yesterday, the city of New York gave me and 60,000 others, the most incredible, warm and inspirational hug I've ever received. What a community!"

> **Life Lesson**
>
> Overcoming the obstacle is the gift.

Chapter Eleven

2019 Tokyo Marathon

> Running makes me strong, resilient, persistent and brave. (Even when I am freezing cold and soaking wet.)

Ten marathons later, everyone (except me) thought I would hang up my running shoes having made it this far. As if that was ever going to happen.

The goal of ten marathons in ten years had finally been achieved.

The Abbott World Marathon Majors series started for me with the 2010 New York Marathon and I had completed it in Boston but then they added Tokyo and I added it to my goals.

Now, I am sitting at my desk at work, forty-eight hours away from finding out if I will secure the last spot on the Travelling Fit team for the 2019 Tokyo Marathon. As usual, I start with the end in mind and visualise myself on 3 March 2019, having completed all six of the Abbott World Marathon Majors series – six amazing marathons.

I am now so close to discovering if this dream, of finally completing the series will become a reality and I wonder if I will get a place. Are the green lights? They have to be.

But I still have so many questions buzzing around my head.

"To run or not to run?"

"Will I do it on my own?" My running friends, who I would normally call upon to run with me, may not be able to run Tokyo this year. So many individual reasons; wanting to do a different race, injuries, the wrong year, work and finances.

"Will I do it without Chad?" He just does not want to go to Tokyo. He has been before and he is not keen to travel with all we have going on at home. I have never run a marathon without him standing on the pavement, waiting with the banner and cheering me on. He calms me down the night before and he came with me to the start line in San Francisco, as he knew it was my first time running a marathon on my own. Running Tokyo would mean training, travelling and running solo.

"No Support Team?" I could be alone in a country where I did not speak the language.

"Why do I want to run Tokyo?" Is it just for a six-star medal, or is it something more?

I have emailed the Abbott World Marathon Majors organisers to double-check my eligibility for the Six Star Medal. It is a massive medal with a picture of all six countries. I am waiting for their response. If they say I am eligible, will that help to make my decision?

I think about why I am so determined to run Tokyo in 2019 and not wait until 2020 when I could potentially run it with Helen and Jerry, who are considering running it next year.

If it is meant to be, it is up to me, runs through my head.

Never let others decide your dreams for you.

Finish what you started.

Back yourself and follow your intuition.

I have five of six stars on the Abbott World Marathon Majors website. I am nearly there, but not quite. I am not a quitter and know that if I can get a place I will go. Who knows what will happen in the future?

All these thoughts had been running through my head and none of us knew then what we know now about what would happen in 2020! The email arrived from the Abbott World Marathon Majors and I will achieve the medal if I get a place and run the distance once more!

Having established I am eligible for the Six Star Medal I contacted Travelling Fit, in 2018, to discuss it with them, as they are the only tour company in Australia that offers entries into this race.

To my utter surprise, when I called them, the 2019 Tokyo Marathon was already full.

I cannot get an entry for 2019, and I want to run it even more. Travelling Fit has placed me on the waitlist, but they will not know if

I can get in, for three to four months. It all depends on someone else making the decision not to run or getting injured. I can enter the lottery, but that is months away and it is one of the most over-subscribed marathons after London. No chance!

I am going to find a way. I talk to lots of people, anyone and everyone I know. I am determined to run this marathon in 2019. I feel like I need to run it, with no idea why. Intuition is an excellent tool if you listen to it. Several friends and colleagues are kind enough to reach out to their networks to see if they can get me an entry, but with no luck.

I believe that you can make big dreams a reality with a successful attitude. I made so many big dreams come true when I was building my business in the UK. I am not giving up.

I will run this race and I have to trust that I will get an entry with the Travelling Fit team. I start telling people I am going and I know I will run it on my own if I have to.

I take a call from Travelling Fit. They might have two places for 2019, but they will not know until Monday. They are just calling to give me the heads up and time to decide.

So here I am sitting at work, forty-eight hours away from finding out if I have an entry. I had a long weekend ahead, wondering if I would run Tokyo and complete my goal. I called my trusted running friends to find out if they want the extra entry (if I get two places) and Helen is out due to work commitments. Jerry is waiting until 2020. Timara, a work colleague, is planning to run New York Marathon. Shelby is out. Ben is out; he is sticking to his running retirement.

If I get the entry, I am going to run and I am going solo if I have to. I am going to run marathon number eleven. I am going to complete what I started. Over the weekend, Chad also agrees (somewhat reluctantly) to come with me if I get a place. I think he is secretly hoping that I do not.

Forty-eight hours have passed and still no phone call. I am beside myself with anxiety, but I do not give up. Tuesday afternoon and finally the call comes. I put the phone down. I now wait for the email to come through just in case I did not hear them correctly. Have you ever kept refreshing your emails every few seconds? I did. I saw the confirmation email pop up on the bottom right-hand corner of my screen; I took a breath and opened it. I am in.

I have an entry. I am now sitting in my office with a big smile. I did not give up on my dream. I made this happen and the bonus is that Chad is coming with me, even if it is reluctantly!

My lunchtime run today is the start of my road to Tokyo. Amazing how a new goal motivates you to get up from your office chair and move. It is a sunny winter's day in Sydney, cool but with a brilliant blue sky. I ran with butterflies in my stomach today, nothing was going to stop me now.

My work colleagues, however, were not so excited.

Teams I have worked with over the years, often dread my lunchtime runs as I head out of the office, only to return an hour later buzzing with what I think are great ideas to increase sales, solve a customer query or just an idea for a campaign.

Running is not only great exercise, but it is my time. There are no distractions or interruptions! Running really does clear my mind in a way that nothing else does. Many people practice meditation and I have tried that but for me, I think running does the same thing. I find that as I run, solutions come to mind.

On one of these runs earlier that same year, I had decided once again it was time for a move – a sea change out of Sydney nearer the coast. Poor Chad!

Training for Tokyo was happening as we sold the house once again, packed it up, bought a new one and rented an apartment in Sydney so that I could continue to work. There is a saying that goes, *"if you want something done, ask a busy person."* It was busy for a few months.

By now though, I knew what to do. I plugged everything into my schedule and got more efficient with my time. I am not sure that I could have handled all of this with the previous marathons, but this one did feel a little easier. Not to diminish the distance at all, it is a very long way, but the training was something that my body was used to by now. I had no doubts (at last) in my post-menopausal mind that, at the age of 59, I could and would cross the finish line of the 2019 Tokyo Marathon. What significant progress I had made with my mind chatter.

We have talked a lot about the gear, the training and the races, but we have yet to speak about feet.

Running really does start with the feet. Or I should say feat.

"Using your feet to achieve amazing feats."

This takes only one small vowel change and running any distance you choose is merely one small transformation. One step becomes two. Take one step, add one step, then add another and so on. It is as simple as that, but I have never said it is easy. It takes determination and consistency.

I have taken good care of my feet, as they are one of the many tools I have needed to make these dreams come true. I have been experimenting with different socks and shoes over the years, but nothing can replace a regular pedicure at home or a salon to take care of the blisters, the hard skin, the bunions and, well, I am sure you do not need me to go into more detail. Suffice it to say, black toenails are a real thing after a marathon. Look after your feet; they will look after you when you run!

Running has been good for my body and mind over the years. When possible, I run on softer surfaces like grass to reduce the impact on my joints and running on softer surfaces allows my body to recover more quickly. I also tend to run with friends and not solo all of the time, as that can be tough. If you are struggling with motivation, try to find a friend to run with you. As well as providing variety to your running, it is excellent for your mental health and safer than running alone.

Having run for over ten years also means I know how my body reacts to the fuel I put into it. I am no saint when it comes to food (or wine), but running has had a huge impact on keeping control of my weight through menopause. This, alone, has also affected my physical and mental health and the scales!

Setting goals for the many races I have completed has increased my self-confidence. This book is about marathons, but I have run numerous other distances in between those races.

I have been asked how I find out about the different events that I have competed in; I tend to find out by accident when a running friend calls and says, "Shall we do this race?" Social media, or the numerous blogs I subscribe to, are also good sources of information. And there are so many different types of races. You can race a train, try to beat a car and do amazing hill races like the annual Balmoral Burn event in Sydney. It does not have to be the marathon distance; it just has to be something that you enjoy.

If you have been inspired to give running (or any other sport a go), be sure to set yourself some realistic goals. This could be running your first kilometre, joining your local parkrun and completing a 5 km walk. Just Google parkrun and you will find the one closest to you. At a parkrun, you will meet like-minded people who want to be active and do crazy races with you.

I did this when I moved to the South Coast around the same time I was training for Tokyo. I found my new community. Sometimes, just showing up pays off. Having goals has helped give me a purpose for my training, a sense of achievement and a medal or two. This is essential for my motivation. You just need to find what works for you.

Running the 2019 Tokyo Marathon was the last one on my goal list. Travelling Fit took control of the planning this time, which was a great relief with everything going on in my life. They took care of the hotel, the pasta party the night before and the logistics around getting to the expo, collecting the bibs and getting to the start line.

All I had to do was run 42.195 km. The camaraderie of this team was great. I need never have worried about running solo as many there were running on their own. Travelling Fit also provided us with great branded running shirts, so everyone running had an instant support crew when the shirts were spotted on the course.

The day of the race was wet – very wet. It poured with rain. I was going to live my worst nightmare of running for hours in the pouring rain. It was going to be my first wet race from start to finish and by now, you know, I do not do the cold very well. I had a tremendous rainproof running jacket that had travelled to all the marathons; today, it was finally coming out of the suitcase. I walked out of the hotel door and I was wet.

Waiting at the start line was horrible. Wet, cold and miserable, I just wanted it all to be over. I had gloves on, ready to discard as I got warmed up. I wore them the whole day. I never warmed up. The challenge of this marathon was to stay motivated despite the cold and the rain. I fixed my sights on that Six Star Medal that would be placed around my neck at the finish line and I ran my heart out.

It was tough, but I stayed focused on running and not overthinking anything else. At about 20 km, I lined up in the toilet queue without realising it was a squat portaloo. Who knew they even existed? That was quite a low point of the race and I will never forget trying to squat with tired legs and then pulling up my very wet Lululemon leggings with cold fingers and wet knickers. The unspoken joys of achieving dreams!

Shortly after this, I saw Chad standing alone in the pouring rain, substituting the banner today with an umbrella. I felt so bad for him. Running in the cold and wet is terrible enough but standing for hours in the pouring rain was a testament to his support.

The cold and fatigue were forgotten in a heartbeat as I crossed the finish line and the 2019 Tokyo Marathon medal was placed around my neck. Moments later, I was in a special corral for Six Star Medal winners. I was ecstatic. I stared at the enormous medal and began to fully comprehend what I had achieved. I only wish I could have shared the moment with Chad, but spectators are not allowed in the finish area.

I felt pure joy and utter relief. It was freezing cold. I was very wet and had tears of joy streaming down my already wet face.

Just when I thought it could not get any better, it did. At the post-race celebrations arranged by Travelling Fit, I met Deena Kastor, a famous female American long-distance runner. I first came across Deena when a group of us went to watch a running documentary,

Spirit of the Marathon in 2007, which follows her victory at the 2005 Chicago Marathon.

After winning the bronze medal in the 2004 Olympic Marathon, she went on to win the 2005 Chicago Marathon. In 2006, she won the London Marathon, setting an American record until Keira D'Amato broke the record in January 2022 (Houston Marathon), taking 24 seconds off with a time of 2:19:12 hours. Deena placed sixth at the 2006 New York City Marathon and fifth at the 2007 Boston Marathon.

Deena had run the marathon that same day in Tokyo (finishing hours in front of me), but that night, she was on stage presenting certificates to every recipient of the Abbott Six Star Medals. As I walked across the stage and got to chat with her for just a few minutes, I knew every step had been worth it and that this was not going to be my last marathon. Deena herself completed the Abbott World Marathon Major Series in Berlin in 2022

Running keeps me on track with life. Aside from my family, running is my life!

> **Life Lesson**
>
> When you back yourself you will achieve amazing feats.

CHAPTER TWELVE

2022 Canberra Marathon

> Running makes me strong, resilient, persistent and brave. (Even when I am freezing cold and soaking wet.)

Three years after the Tokyo Marathon, I find myself training for the 2022 Canberra Marathon. As we all know, most races and events were cancelled in 2020 and 2021. My deferred 2020 entry for the Australian Outback Marathon in the heart of Australia had to be cancelled again in 2021 when the state borders closed and I could not get to Uluru.

Running the 2022 Canberra Marathon was a direct result and silver lining, of being in isolation on the Far South Coast of NSW during the COVID-19 pandemic. It was never on my list of goals or even on my radar as I had been commuting to Sydney for over a year when the pandemic hit and had little time for much else. Within weeks of the pandemic announcement, I had closed the office and was working from home on the Far South Coast of NSW. As we all went into a COVID coma and a stay-at-home existence, I was now forced to plant my feet firmly in this regional town that I found myself in 24/7.

I was no longer a drive-in-drive-out resident and I missed my city life of cafes and cinemas, my weekly runs with mates and the shopping. But then, so did everyone. Slowing down was a challenge and weirdly eerie. Work was crazy, with hours spent in front of a computer monitor and I launched myself into a self-imposed pandemic productivity challenge.

At the end of each working day, there were no theatres or restaurants to unwind in; no catch-ups with friends after work. I felt somewhat lost and cut off, as I am sure most of the country and the rest of the world did. Netflix became my new best friend and I got cosy at home with too many wines and home-cooked food. I even turned my hand to making pasta, which was a massive fail and gave me hours of unwanted cleaning in the kitchen.

Months passed and I needed to change how I dealt with isolation (or iso, as the Australians like to call it).

The following months in my iso cocoon were spent running on my own. I have been running for over ten years now and found that wherever I am in the world, I can lace up my shoes and head out for a run. It has been my solace. Now I was at home, doing the same thing again.

Running was my time away from endless Zoom meetings. It was my time to find solutions for issues at work, de-stress, move more and sow seeds for the next running goal, whenever that might be. As a marathon runner, I usually work towards the next race, but with the world, in a coma, there were no face-to-face events and the virtual ones were not inspiring me.

One of my new running goals, at this time, was trail running.

My running so far has been in the city, around the streets and suburbs where I had lived. But now that I was living on the coast, I discovered a new joy: the fantastic bush trails and coastal paths. Running solo and walking the amazing beaches near home, I started listening to my podcasts and books again. I also spent time trying to discover if I had green fingers. I do not. Running locally, I slowly discovered the beauty around me and I felt privileged to be isolated on the Far South Coast, where I could do this. Others were not so lucky.

As the world began to emerge from this "iso" state, I knew I needed to reach out to the local running community. Having made the sea change just before COVID, I did not know any runners, so I turned to my local parkrun in Batemans Bay. I knew no one. I had run a few parkrun's in Sydney but never consistently and never really met anyone.

Each week I showed up at Batemans Bay and gradually I met a few like-minded people. Joining the parkrun community made it easy and I gingerly joined a local running group as a result.

That first Sunday, as I joined the local trail running group, I was out of my *"depth, my running depth."* As I circled Wagonga Lake near Narooma, I remember hearing the bellbirds calling, seeing the blue lake sparkling and the oyster beds spreading far and wide. It was an absolutely stunning run, but I could run no further.

At the 20 km mark, Chad was parked on the fire trail, just in case I needed a pickup, so I bailed out of the run early. Crossing this beautiful rickety old bridge over a creek where some kids were playing, I just could not keep up with the new group and thought that would be the last time I saw them. The shame of not completing the run would have stopped me from returning the following week.

That is when I met Ren for the first time. She stopped as well. A total stranger, Ren jumped into the car and said, "Thank goodness. I need a ride to the finish." This made me drive to the finish point and not straight home, as I am sure I would have done if it had not been for her. Welcomed by the running group at the end of the trail, we sat by the water eating locally caught fish and chips, another reason to live where I do. The chatter was refreshingly normal and welcoming and I finally began to breathe.

As I embraced this local community, I met more and more people at parkrun. I discovered the beauty of the running trails along the coastline, local coffee spots and hidden cafes away from the hustle and bustle of city life. Whales swim close to the coastline and seals live on the local rocks. I formed friendships founded on the shared anxieties of the recent and ongoing events in the world – fear and fun in a weird period of history.

I found my running wings again; what started at the local parkrun, led to sharing a ride with one runner and then to running the Canberra Marathon with the running group from the Far South Coast.

Lisa, a new running friend, had never run a marathon before and she decided that she was going to train for Canberra. I decided to support her with the training and then run it with her. That is how I came to find myself running the 2022 Canberra Marathon.

Lisa was new to marathon running, so I went back to basics with her. It reminded me of how many questions I get asked about running, so whilst I have always said this is not a technical book, I will dive into some of the nitty-gritty of running (according to me) that you might not find in other running books.

To begin training for a full marathon, you need to start with a good solid base and I do not mean just a good physical running base.

You need a good mental base as well. Focusing on improving your attitude toward running (and life) will get you through some of the tougher parts of training and running the distance of a marathon. If you decide not to run in the rain, the cold, when it is dark, when you feel tired and the list goes on, you will find completing a marathon impossible.

The way I deal with this is to simply tell myself, *"It is going to be ok!"*

It is ok to run in the rain. It might be cold, but you can have a hot shower afterwards. The soreness will ease and the tiredness will make the run slower than usual, but "It will be ok."

Choose your attitude for the next sixteen weeks; it will help with your running and change your life. It did mine when I crossed the finish line of my first marathon in Paris in 2009.

The solid physical base could be a few months of regular running (unless you are my son, Ben, of course)! Running three times a week at a steady pace and completing 10 km with some sort of ease will help with the months of training ahead. When Helen and I decided to run Paris, we had completed a 9 km race and a half marathon and had been running for just over a year.

I also believe that healthy eating contributes to my running success, but I have never counted calories or the number of grams of protein I need, as I am sure many runners do and many find it useful. I just eat good food (and some bad as well).

I have talked a lot about the training schedule and fitting everything in, week by week, but there are hundreds of marathon plans. Every marathon I have trained for has been different because I have rarely used the same schedule twice and everyone will recommend a different one. I have used ones from books, the internet and programmes designed by coaches. They all work. Marathon schedules use a lot of jargon when it comes to training and they will feature words you may have never heard of like fartlek, intervals and tempo runs.

Fartlek training is playing around with speeds – essentially, it is a form of unstructured speedwork. It involves a continuous run in which periods of faster running are mixed with periods of easy or moderately paced running, not complete rest, as with interval training. Fartlek workouts are a great way to introduce quicker or more intense running into your routine.

Interval training is a form of speedwork designed to get you used to running at faster speeds and when used well, it can do wonders for your fitness and speed. This is how I started running that first cold winter evening when I showed up at the oval. Interval training means you run fast for a while, rest for a short period and then run fast again. I still do them regularly and I still find them challenging.

A tempo run means that you run at a steady tempo or pace (as runners like to call it) for a longer distance. It is whatever feels comfortable to you. It is conversation pace – my favourite pace. Then, there is the long run. I always remember Coach Fi telling us that the long run was the most important part of the training. She used to tell us to sacrifice any other run in the week if it was going to mean that we could not do the long run. The long run is the run that gets longer and longer and longer and longer every week of the training. Building up muscle memory (slowly) is important and will help to get you to the finish line with as few injuries as possible.

Building up the distances too quickly will lead to injury. As a rule of thumb, we added 2 km each week until we were running 30+ km. a few times before race day.

Another critical aspect of the long run is taking in fuel as you run. Once again, it is very personal, but you cannot run a full marathon (unless you want to hit the mythical wall) without eating as you run. Hence, the training is about finding out what you like to eat on a run and, more importantly, what your stomach can tolerate. As previously mentioned, I have used the standard liquid running gels you buy at any good running store, but I got very fed up with the gooey texture and after a few marathons, I just could not consume them anymore. The gels also come in a cube, tasting much like a jelly sweet but with added electrolytes, so I have switched to them. Whatever works for you (including sandwiches), it is essential to eat them during the long-run training. Remember, it is best to avoid anything new on race day.

Most marathon training schedules will be based on similar concepts and some good research online and you will find one that suits you. The training schedule we used for the Canberra Marathon was different to previous ones and was taken from a concept called Run Less Run Smarter. I was not going to risk injury this time. Google it if you are interested. Over the years, I have also incorporated yoga and swimming into my training routine to help with my fitness and flexibility and this programme had lots of cross training like this.

My race day gear is the first thing I pack when I am travelling to an event. I lay it all out on the bed to ensure I have not forgotten anything, including my race day undies. I start with shoes and socks and work my way up to the hat. This includes my running watch (and charger) and even my hair band to tie my hair up with. I leave nothing to chance.

This way, I know I have everything. The night before the race, I lay it all out again (usually on the hotel floor) because I know that on the morning of the race, I will be so nervous that I could forget anything. I pack my fuel in my running belt, pin my bib onto my race day top and prepare my breakfast banana and bagel. I love my coffee before a run (it helps with the pre-race bathroom visit) and I always pack individually wrapped coffee bags. Races often start very early and you cannot guarantee finding coffee then. I leave nothing to chance.

It takes me precisely 30 minutes from the time I get up, to be ready for a race. I need my sleep and the pre-race nerves mean that my sleep has usually been interrupted, so I have fined tuned the morning routine. We always ensure that we know precisely how to get to the start line and usually practice getting there the day before, so we can get there with just enough time to join the long queues for the portaloo. You may have been to the bathroom many times before you leave your accommodation, but you will still need that last nervous 'wee' before the marathon!

Then it is time to line up in your designated corral. The training is complete. The wait is over. The atmosphere is so exciting. It is electric. The runners are buzzing and everyone is taking photos and selfies to mark this momentous occasion. The weeks of training and hard work have all been for this moment in time and the butterflies in my stomach are always present and flying.

The 2022 Canberra Marathon was no different from any other marathon except that I was now with a new running community from my new home on the Far South Coast. We had all met up the previous evening for a "carb" loading dinner, with no food poisoning, only nervous chatter and race day conversations. My daughter, Shelby, still living overseas, flew in for the race once again. This time, however, her fiancé is running as well. I am not sure that we can call this a ripple effect of running, but Shelby's fiancé is not just a runner but a fast runner. Shelby now spends much of her time supporting him at running events. Like father, like daughter.

Race day was chilly as we headed towards the start line in the dark. Lisa and a few others were first-timers, but most had run a marathon before and so knew what to expect. Group photos complete, we lined up in the streets of Australia's capital. It was unlike the big international marathons, with music pumping and massive crowds cheering as the starting gun went off but it felt perfect to me. Chatting with Lisa, who was so nervous, surrounded by my new running community and running in the same event as my future son-in-law. Chad and Shelby were our support crew once again, and now joined by Ren, who had made me feel so welcome just months previously.

Running the streets of Canberra was magnificent, around new Parliament House, Old Parliament House and the beautiful lake. The support crew from the Far South Coast were there and it was fabulous to see so many new, yet familiar faces on the course, cheering us all on every step of the way. For me, it was a slow marathon, but thankfully uneventful. Recovering from COVID just weeks previously, I was not going to push myself having had interrupted training once again. I knew I could finish and that was enough for me. Family, new friends and old surrounded me. There was no self-doubt.

Lisa and I did not run together on race day. We ran our own race at our own pace. We saw each other on the course; as there were many twists and turns, back loops and switchbacks. I finished hours after my soon-to-be son-in-law, who was showered and back at the finish line when I finally completed the 2022 Canberra Marathon in a little over five hours. The time was irrelevant. Living only two hours away, we all headed home and the post-race celebrations went well into the night in my back garden with champagne flowing and stories of the day told and re-told.

Running my twelfth marathon felt just like I was back in Paris running my first one.

I had run full circle and it was more than OK!

> **Life Lesson**
> When you take small steps to try something new, it moves you in the right direction.

Conclusion - The Ripple Effects of Running

> *My dream is for every reader to experience the thrill of the finishing line, the journey it takes to get there, the friends you make along the way and the inner strength that never fades.*

The ripple effects of my running are woven throughout the chapters of this book. They are many and they have been life changing.

To put into words what running means to me is the hardest part of this book. Finding the right words to fully describe and convey my passion and what it has done for me and can do for you is harder than running the 42.195 km of a full marathon.

What started on a cold winter night in July 2007 was a journey that impacted every aspect of my life, including family, friends and friends of friends. Running twelve marathons, numerous half marathons and some crazy races through glowworm tunnels and up mountains has spilt over into all aspects of my life.

One of the most significant ripple effects of running is being part of a running community. Big or small and forever changing, my running community spans from local runners to global runners. From friends, I know well to the spectators who have supported every event I have participated in. I could not have experienced the thrill and exhilaration of crossing so many finishing lines without every one of them.

The running community has been my therapist in life. They may not have the formal qualifications that a college course provides, but they have listened, helped and assisted me through many of life's significant events over the past fifteen years. From empty nesting, redundancies, health crises and everyday work stress, I sometimes think they know me better than anyone. The running conversations have been my life support.

Living thousands of miles away from most of my family, I have confided in my running mates. I have asked for advice and sought answers to questions I had no one else to ask. The unspoken code of *"what goes on a run, stays on the run"* has enabled me to share my innermost thoughts and anxieties, often finding out that they are not unique to me but shared by many.

Running has a major ripple effect on your physical health, but in my mind, the massive mental and emotional benefits far outweigh that. Running with like-minded individuals week in and week out builds a considerable level of trust between you, allowing for the authenticity of conversations without any judgement.

If we are honest, we have probably all experienced imposter syndrome, self-doubt and anxiety at one point or another in our careers. My strong mental wellbeing has been a major ripple effect of running on all levels. Work, family and relationship issues; there is little that cannot be discussed with a bunch of women on a 30 km long run.

The effect of running has been immeasurable for my family. My gratitude for Chad's 100% support of my passion – some would call it an addiction – is hard to put into words. He has spent hours cycling around streets trying to find me on a training run, only to be greeted by a grumpy runner demanding food and water. He has sat through way too many running dinners when all we talk about is the last run or the next run. He has cooked Spaghetti Carbonara for me most Friday nights before my long run to ensure I am fully fueled. He has supported every event I have competed in, holding the banner and wearing his lime green crazy shirt so that we can easily spot him in the crowd of spectators. He has spent hours on the pavement trying to spot me in a mass of runners as we run by, only to miss me on many occasions.

He stood for over five hours in the rain during the Tokyo Marathon and only managed to see me pass by once. When we finally met up at the end of the race, I was so cold, wet, tired and hangry that I was snappy and ungrateful, to say the least. Even though that was the marathon where I achieved the World Major Marathons Medal, I remember the two of us sitting in the hotel room that night and ordering room service. It had been such a tough day.

His sacrifices are endless and way too many to mention, but he has never complained. Running has given us the space we need in our relationship when I am pounding the streets for hours on end and sleeping on a Saturday afternoon. Running has bonded us because of Chad's unwavering support and dedication. Soon to celebrate forty years of marriage, running has, without a doubt, been a contributing factor to our solid and lasting relationship.

Running the 2017 New York Marathon with Shelby and Ben was simply the best. A cumulation of ten years of them being on the sidelines of my running.

Shelby flew around the world to spectate and support me at so many events, watching from the sidelines with her dad, my number one fan. Shelby started to run and we have shared many a great hour running around the iconic Cremorne Point in Sydney together. She was first to spring into action when the Boston bomb went off that day when I had called her at such an early hour.

I will never forget running with her the morning after Chad's stroke, after a long night spent at the hospital. As Shelby and I arrived home, she asked what I wanted to do. She knew the answer before I had uttered a word. Shelby wanted to go for breakfast, but she came for a run with me first.

I would regularly creep out of the house at 5 am on a Saturday, leaving the house full of Ben's mates usually hungover, sleeping it off and I only knew how many had stayed the previous night by the number of shoes outside the front door. Returning mid-morning, I would find them sitting around, drinking coffee, but they were always interested in my run and appeared to be in awe of the distances. This had to have had a lasting effect on Ben. I think this sowed the marathon seed; Ben just did not know it yet.

Sharing my tenth marathon in ten years with Shelby and Ben still fills me with tears of emotion. I know what it takes to get to the start line and they trained for months to make that happen. The day was fun; we laughed, shared stories and solved a few problems along the 42.195 km route. Crossing the finish line, collecting our medals and struggling to walk the next day are all priceless memories we share because I lace up my shoes and head out of the front door. None of this was planned. No goals were set for this to happen and it makes me believe that if you just give it a go, you might surprise yourself with what you can achieve, much as I did.

My niece, Steph, had been a spectator for my first marathon in Paris when Nigel, her dad and my inspiration for running, had driven the minibus of family supporters through the Channel Tunnel from the UK to Paris. A few years later, Steph travelled to Australia for her Gap Year and came to live with us for a few months. By the time she returned home to the UK, she had run with us on Saturday mornings, joined the KTP post-run breakfast club and caught the running bug. Steph went on to run a full marathon in Bath and is still trying to get an entry into the London Marathon.

I have made amazing lifelong friends within the running community and you will too. I have shared experiences, highs and lows – working towards a common goal will do that. When I met Helen on that first night of running with Can Too in July 2007, I never dreamed that we would achieve all that we have, despite both having successful careers and living in different States for much of the time.

Chad and I now live on the Far South Coast of NSW because Helen and David have a beach house there and they introduced us to their friends and family. Another running ripple is that one of Chad's best mates is now David, Helen's husband. We have travelled the world with them and had many laughs together, mainly when David leaves his mobile in an airport terminal or drops it down a portaloo in a race.

I am so lucky to have so many friends still in my life because of running. I am sure I would have lost contact with Marie, that work colleague from Utah if it was not for shared runs in the beautiful mountains outside Salt Lake City before a conference.

Timara and I worked together for just two years, but in that time, she started running. We ran along the Brisbane River one day before work for 20 km and I had no idea she had never run that far. Timara went on to run the New York Marathon and we still catch up from time to time for a quick 5 km run. Two of our original running group, Anu and Andrew, now live in London and we got to stay with them recently on a trip back to the UK and ran along the river Thames together. It was perfect. The ripple list goes on.

We are now part of the Far South Coast running crew where we share new runs and experiences. When Lisa decided to train for the Canberra Marathon the ripple effect of that, went through the local running group, with many choosing to do the same event and once again, we found ourselves travelling to a running event, as we have done so many times before. This time with new friends, Chad and Shelby spectating and me running in the same event as my future son-in-law. We are making new running memories and enjoying new trail-running events.

These currently include a whole variety of other distances like the Coastal Classic, a 30 km trail run held in the Royal National Park NSW and running the new Bondi to Manly Ultra, an 80 km race, as a relay team.

I have stepped down from full-time work, but all those hours of running and the new ideas that come to me will not be wasted as I move into the next stage of my life. I will be able to spend more time with Chad and run more. I will continue to run wherever I am, but now I will share the learnings on stage so that more women are inspired to move more, one step at a time.

Running has cost me a small fortune in shoes, clothes, race entries, travel, running watches, physiotherapy, massages, books on running and, well, the list is long and as Chad might read this one day, I will leave the list there, but running has repaid me in dividends beyond my wildest dreams.

Running has changed me physically. It has kept me fit, helped me cope with menopause and motivated me to eat well and drink less. Running with a hangover is no fun! I have great energy and my new running community have me ocean swimming and setting new goals to learn to surf in my 60s.

Running has changed me mentally. It has given me the space and time to think things through, providing clarity when contemplating a crucial decision. Running has increased my confidence and belief in myself. I know I can run 42.195 km and because of this, I can dig deep to get the job done, when I face challenging issues at work and home. Running has given me the edge.

Running has strengthened my resilience muscle, knowing that a bad run can be just that, a bad run. A bad day at work can be just that; a bad day at work. I have stopped over-analysing every training and every marathon, which has now made running and doing life a whole lot easier.

The running ripple effect on me as a mum, wife, friend, family member and leader can be summed up in one simple sentence:

I am a better human because I run.

And in the words of Rob de Castella AO MBE

> We may run in circles ending up back where we started, but when we get back, we are not the same person we were.

Acknowledgements

My thanks to the following awesome people who have been part of the running journey and helped me write this book.

Thank you, Anna, who convinced me I was capable of writing. Anna, who was my accountability coach and editor. Anna, who red-penned my first few chapters (a lot) and Anna, who stayed up brainstorming titles by herself late at night.

Thank you, Chad, for your unconditional support and sacrifice over the years of my running and on our European holiday when I took time out (a lot) to get started on this project. Thank you for never complaining about the money we spent on the marathons. Thank you for being a barista.

Thank you, Shelby and Ben, for running New York with me. It was and always will be very precious. It is my favourite chapter in the book. Shelby, you have flown around the world to support me at so many races; thank you. Thank you for marrying a runner. Ben, your support and belief in me in writing this book mean a great deal.

Thank you, Steph (and Dave), for looking after Charlie while Helen and I ran.

Thank you, Fiona, for being a great coach and being tough, "tellsomeonewhocares.com," but most of all, thank you for the race entries.

Thank you, KTP (Keep the Pace), my first running group. Jerry, the maps, the music and London. Julie, for the thongs in Chicago. Peita, your story from New York made me cry. Thank you for sharing it. Andrew and Anu, we miss running with you. Time to come home.

Thank you, Mark (The Body Mechanic), for getting me to the start line of so many races.

Thank you, Allana, for introducing me to Anna, reading the chapters and asking some great questions that the readers now have answered.

Thank you, Julie, for your support (you know who you are).

Thank you, Ren, for jumping in my car that day.

Thank you, my second running group, SLR (Sunday Long Run), for introducing me to the Far South Coast running trails. For waiting for me on every run. Ensuring I see sunrises.

Thank you, George, for teaching me the personal development I have used in work and running. For believing in me and allowing me to run your company in Australia.

Thank you, Travelling Fit, for getting me that last entry into Tokyo Marathon.

Thank you, Can Too, for running that advertisement.

And a MASSIVE

Thank you to Helen (and David). The journey would not have been the same without you both. This journey would not have happened and I would not have written this book. It is because of you both that I now get to live my best life on the Far NSW South Coast.

About the Author

Gillian Stapleton is a renowned leader and has led multinational global organisations and Australian-based not for profits. An entrepreneur at heart, Gillian has run her own business, served on Boards and is passionate about empowering others, particularly women, to be the best they can be by finding their true passion and thriving.

Gillian has an infectious personality both on stage and in the boardroom. Goal-driven, Gillian has taken many risks in life, not least that of running her first marathon at the age of 49. Since then, she has completed 12 marathons (to date) and is a holder of the World Majors Marathon medal. The ripple effect of running on her life, how she overcame many challenges as a result, and the amazing friendships she has made are what Gill is most proud of.

When Gillian is not running, she now spends her time working with businesses, inspiring women to be the best version of themselves.

Connect with Gillian through Instagram @RunningCircles42

@RUNNINGINCIRCLES42

www.ingramcontent.com/pod-product-compliance
Lightning Source LLC
Chambersburg PA
CBHW030257010526
44107CB00053B/1746